ELLE JAE

What is Cryptocurrency!? An Easy Beginner's Guide on How to Invest and the Future of Digital Currencies

Disclaimer:

Please note that the information provided in this book is intended to be used for educational purposes only and should not be relied upon as legal, accounting or financial advice. The crypto market is highly volatile and investing involves a lot of risk, so it is key to understand that past performances of an asset is not always a guarantee for future sways of the market. Elle Jae is not responsible for any losses or financial gains and it is highly recommended for all readers to do their own analysis before investing based on personal circumstances.

First edition

ISBN: 9798455245695

Illustration by Danny Perdana (outerheavendarkart@gmail.com)
Editing by Andrea Leeth (andrea.leeth@gmail.com)

This book was professionally typeset on Reedsy.
Find out more at reedsy.com

This book is dedicated to my mother and late father
- the OG investor and my inspiration.

Contents

Foreword

"An investment in knowledge pays the best interest."

- Benjamin Franklin

Before reading any further, pat yourself on your back and take a moment to appreciate that you have taken a step towards achieving financial freedom. Whether your job, relationship or living situation is bringing you stress, a common goal amongst many people is the desire to become financially secure. This can stem from wanting to own your dream home, a fancy car or to simply take care of your family and give back to those in need. Whatever the reason, let the imagination of your financial end goal burn a fiery passion inside to drive you through this new chapter of your life.

A huge part of mentally preparing yourself for financial freedom is the belief that it can be achieved. It really saddens me to read posts online of people limiting themselves with doubt, due to the fact that they have a misconception that people who are successful originally come from money. The *World Ultra Wealth Report* published in 2019 revealed that; 67.7% of the world's richest people were self-made, 23.7% had a mix of inherited and self-created wealth, whilst only 8.5% of high-net-worth individuals worldwide are classified as having inherited their fortune entirely. These figures are quite inspiring to dwell on as it shows that the majority of the wealthiest people are indeed self-made.

One misconception when it comes to investing in cryptocurrency is that you need to have a hefty savings in order to start investing. A fun fact is that if you invested only $1 in Bitcoin back in July 2010 and did not sell until 2021, you would have an astonishing $800,000! You don't need an arm and a leg to start investing within the crypto space and that fact alone is why investing in the market has become so popular.

From party girl status to being a successful crypto investor, I am living proof that you don't need to be born into generational wealth or have to attend a prestigious university with a business, finance or economics degree to be a prominent investor. My thirst for knowledge and craving to be financially secure led me to crypto, which has honestly changed my life and has allowed me to get rid of a lot of financial burdens that were weighing me down. As a result, this book was written in hopes of inspiring those who are willing to take the next financial step in their life to realise that you too can do the same.

Our beliefs alone can be a blessing or a curse since our actions are an extension of the thoughts that go on in our minds. An example of a damaging mindset towards financial freedom appeared during a conversation during the 2020 pandemic, which geared around my friend feeling uncertain about being financially stable. When I asked him what actions he was taking to try and overcome this uncertainty, he confidently responded by saying that he will win the lottery and get rich that way.

I thought he was being sarcastic, but he was truly serious. I responded by questioning how he expects to win since he doesn't buy lottery tickets, and how this logic alone can be destructive to his growth. Simply put, if you're not willing to put in the work, then you will not reap the rewards – otherwise, these thoughts remain a fantasy rather than making it into a reality. Moving forward, this negligent way of thinking cannot be applied to any investment because you need to be confident with your portfolio, otherwise you will be gambling with your hard-earned money. Luckily for you, I have saved you a long time doing research and have condensed everything that you will need to know into this simplistic beginner's guide. All you can do from here on out is take notes along the way, implement your research and believe that you too can change your life for the better by becoming an investor.

1

Global Financial Issues that Led to Cryptocurrency

"It is well enough that people of the nation do not understand
our banking and monetary system,
for if they did,
I believe there would be a revolution before tomorrow morning."

— Henry Ford

Before diving into an explanation of what cryptocurrency is, we need to deconstruct the value of what money truly is to understand the fundamental flaws of the traditional financial system that sparked the inception of cryptocurrencies. The generalisation of how money retains value gets overlooked due to this subject not being taught in schools or casually discussed in typical passing conversations. Consequently, the concept of money was just something that was widely accepted that we wouldn't question. That was the case for me at least, which I assume many readers would also be in the same boat.

If we break down the functionality of money, the basis is built as a means of exchange for goods and services, a measure of value while also being a store of value. Instead of lugging around gold bars back in the day in exchange for goods and services, the model changed to trusting financial institutions to solve this problem by printing fiat money (legal tender) bills and coins out of convenience. The repetitive money cycle is that at a job, we offer our time and hard work in exchange for fiat, where our boss can't stamp our earnings on a random piece of paper because it's not a trusted source of value. Fiat money has value because our society is built upon *trust* where it can be exchanged for goods and services.

As boring as this may be for some, it's quite fascinating to dwell on the fact that our money only has value because we give it value. If one day the government started issuing Pokémon cards and deems the holographic Charizard card as a value of £1000, then we would use it to exchange for goods and services based on the foundation of *trust*. Obviously, that is a ridiculous comparison, but hopefully you get the point. The essence of money is derived from those who make fiat centralised - controlled and unlimited.

Until 1971, countries had to print their fiat money based on the gold held in reserves, which restricted infinite money printing. When President Nixon abolished the Gold Standard that year, this allowed central banks to print

2

money out of thin air. Pantera Capital CEO Dan Morehead stated in a letter to investors released on July 29th 2020, that the United States printed more money in June 2020 than the first two centuries after its founding. He stated that this was greater than the total debt incurred between 1776 and the end of 1979 and goes on to state, "that's EXACTLY why one should get out of paper money and into Bitcoin. It isn't being inflated away. One bitcoin is a constant fraction of the total 21 million that will ever exist. There is no need for inflation-adjusted numbers — because there is no inflation/hyper-inflation."

When more money is put into circulation, the value drops and the price of goods and services can increase. Once a breach of trust has been made, then the trust starts to fade away and a prime example of this is the hyperinflation crisis happening in Venezuela. The country has the highest inflation rates in the entire world derived from President Nicolás Maduro printing more money into the economy to cover debt, which inconsequentially devalued Venezuela's currency by 96%. The currency is so worthless that there are photos online of paper money flooding the streets, handbags being woven out of bills to sell for profit and garbage bags full of the bills that people don't even want to touch because their fiat money lost its value.

The enticing rise of Bitcoin is decentralisation, which cuts financial institutions out of the picture to never manipulate or add inflation upon the digital currency, while also solving the barbaric system in place for transporting money. It is shocking to think that although we live in a digital age, the banking system that we heavily rely on fails to evolve from the structure in place from 100 years ago. The cost of sending money internationally, for instance through banks, has high fees and takes hours or even days for transfers to hit the other account. Whereas, sending an email or text to someone halfway around the world is instant. Many might assume that this has no effect on themselves because they don't send money internationally, however, this heavily affects businesses (which you could be a consumer of) that have to factor these costs within their prices for goods and services.

In order to fix the traditional financial problems presented above, certain cryptocurrencies came swooping in as Superman to offer an alternative and innovative solution.

2

Crash Course on Crypto and Blockchain Technology

"What are you gonna tell your kids and your grandkids, 25 years from now, when they say 'gee daddy, gee grandpa, what were you doing other than having your thumb up your big fucking ass' during the greatest transformation of wealth in the history of the world? Fucking nothing! That's what most of you will tell them."

- Billionaire, Dan Peña

T he best way to imagine cryptocurrency and blockchain technology is to compare it to the internet before it became a globally accepted adoption. The coding zeros and ones that once seemed too technical for the average Joe to use, has evolved into a distributed information system that our society cannot live a day without for business, social, educational and personal reasons. Although the sector is still fairly new, within the next decade certain cryptocurrencies and blockchain technologies will be used on an international scale in an instinctive manner just like the internet. Precisely how the internet revolutionised communication, decentralised finance (DeFi) is revolutionising traditional finance on an international scale.

Although there is a lot of information on the internet trying to explain the sector that will make your brain feel like it is melting, it doesn't have to be painful to learn. The next few pages will simplify the technicalities by using unique analogies to favourably put it all into perspective. You will be golden if you can get through the next few pages and I guarantee that the sector will get more interesting from here on out.

What is Cryptocurrency?

Let's first split the word cryptocurrency into two parts - crypto and currency.

Crypto is in reference to using cryptography, which is a fancy way of electronically transmitting and storing data with an algorithm, while *currency* is used as a medium of exchange. Referencing back to the previous chapter of how a currency is built on trust, you can look at cryptocurrency as an umbrella term for a trusted currency that is digital. When the two parts are put together, it means that cryptocurrency is a digitally secure currency that is a decentralised medium of exchange. Read the sentence again, but slower to truly gasp what each word represents:

Cryptocurrency is a *digitally secure* currency that is a *decentralised* medium of exchange.

To smoothen over any confusion, it is easier to deconstruct that sentence based on the 3 fundamental elements - decentralisation, transparency and security.

Although money can be digital in a sense that we can view our debit balance online and send money electronically through our bank accounts, cryptocurrency must not be confused with these centralised methods of payments and means of storing value. This is due to banks still having control over various fees, ability to reject opening a bank account, interception of transactions and most importantly, a centralised banking authority uses the money in our private bank accounts as loans to other customers. When there is an act of monetary exchange in a decentralisation manner, there is no central authority involved to act as the middleman to meddle in any financial manner. This cuts all the unnecessary third parties involved for a transaction.

If I wanted to send money abroad to a friend through a centralised banking system for instance, the money would not be sent instantly due to the bank having to meddle in to add its stamp of approval. This creates a very timely and costly process. Through a decentralised system, a transaction goes straight from account A to account C, without the need of it filtering through a middleman (account B) for approval before the money hits the destined account. Contrastingly, the ability to send an email halfway across the world has been easily accessible and instantaneous since the inception of dial up internet, yet the ability to cater to our financial needs, remains a barbaric system from the past.

If I wanted to send an email through Gmail for instance, the server doesn't intercept emails for approval before it reaches the recipient's inbox. This is a similar concept when it comes to the strengths of a decentralised financial network since the sophisticated coding connects the two parties together to cut out the unnecessary baggage of a middleman. This allows transactions to be quicker, transparent, reliable and cheaper. To add transparency and security to decentralised transactions, every transaction is also broadcasted to the entire network that is available on a public ledger, which is usually kept private by banks. This creates a strong ecosystem since it would be highly difficult to cheat the system, which ultimately makes the data immutable. As alarming as this may seem, the public ledger does not contain people's identities, but is rather an anonymous way of tracking the volumes of value being moved of the limited supply of the cryptocurrency. The decentralisation, security and transparency that was lacking within the modern banking system is a pivotal reason for the creation of Bitcoin, and the innovation behind this FinTech revolution is called *blockchain technology*.

What is Blockchain Technology?

The best way to explain blockchain technology is to compare it to how the internet needs WiFi to function. The same premise relates to blockchain technology by being the heart of Bitcoin and various cryptocurrencies – without the heart, the system wouldn't work. The *block* aspect refers to information being stored on multiple ledgers and the *chain* element is a metaphor to link the information together on the system. Confused? Stay with me.

Imagine going out for a day of errands and after each purchase you get a receipt (a block) that has a thread (chain) attached to the previous receipt. At the end of the day, you have multiple receipts linked together by a thread where you can hang up on your wall to view all of your transactions in your order. This is the basis of what blockchain technology is, except instead of collecting information for a day, the transactions are recorded for every single transaction made since the networks' inception.

The barbaric method of using a ledger within banks was to write every transaction down into a physical book, which was then changed to a private database file on a system. These options are not ideal in a fast-growing digital age and as a result, blockchain technology is revolutionising the ancient system due to a system built on accessible trust for a fraction of the price and in a timely manner.

A "Proof-of-Work" (PoW) blockchain is where a feasible amount of effort is needed in order for a "block" to be approved every 10 minutes. Just in the real world where miners dig for gold, cryptos that use PoW require miners in a cryptographic way to have computers linked on the same network to compete against each other to approve transactions. The foundation of various miners approving the transactions creates a trusted and secure network that is difficult to hack, which also reduces fraud. This does not mean as an investor that you will have to be a miner, unless you want to, but this is simply what happens within the system behind closed doors when you buy, send or sell cryptocurrencies that use a proof-of-work blockchain such as Bitcoin.

Although the foundation of blockchain technology was initially designed to power Bitcoin, the system is so versatile that many other sectors are using the technology as an accessible database of information for any source of value or property within the health care sector and even within elections for casting votes. The author of *Blockchain Revolution* Don Tapscott, is very adamant on the technology and is a leading blockchain figure in the digital sphere. His two-million plus viewed TedTalk titled, *How the Blockchain is Changing Money and Business*, is a highly recommended 18:49 minute video on YouTube.

He boldly stated, "I've been at this for 35 years writing about the digital age. I've never seen a technology that I thought had greater potential for humanity." Listening to him speak is very interesting and I'd highly recommend taking the time to search his lectures on YouTube for him to paint a picture of what the future of money and business holds.

The Million Dollar Question - What is Bitcoin (BTC)?

If I had a Bitcoin every time someone asked me what Bitcoin was, I would have retired at 27 instead of 31 on my own private beach sipping margaritas.

Bitcoin was stemmed from the 2007-2008 financial crisis that was deemed as the worst financial crisis since the great depression. It was created to change how money can be managed in a decentralised manner to pioneer a new method for how money can be exchanged and created a new store of value. With the anonymity of the network, lower fees, faster transactions (10 minutes) and not having banks control our wealth, is the momentous reason why there is a lot of trust and value with the digital asset. To this day, the creator of Bitcoin remains anonymous under the mysterious pseudonym of Satoshi Nakamoto. It is usually effective with investments to know the team behind a certain project which adds credibility before investing, but the fact that the creator(s) is not public knowledge, is not actually a negative flaw, but rather an intriguing element that is overshadowed by the trusted technology.

Due to Bitcoin's Proof-of-Work blockchain, a new "block" gets created every 10 minutes for miners to approve transactions, which changes the supply in circulation. When it comes to Bitcoin specifically, there will only ever be 21 million digital coins in existence. This will never change due to the algorithm set in stone which ultimately means that inflation cannot happen with cryptocurrencies that have a capped supply. For example, there are currently 18,408,213 (87.816%) Bitcoins in circulation when writing this in 2020, which only leaves 2,558,575 coins left to be mined. In addition, only 900 Bitcoins are currently mined every day, which cuts in half every 4 years. This positions 2140 to be the final year the last Bitcoin will ever be mined.

Due to the current mined amount of Bitcoin being limited to 900 a day, this causes a supply and demand scare within the market due to institutions now joining the bandwagon in 2020 since it was only retail investors beforehand.

As a result, it was reported in October 2020 that PayPal bought 70% of the newly mined Bitcoin supply since entering the market the same month. This leaves other institutions and retail investors scrambling to get their hands on the remaining supply as institutional interest increases, which creates a supply shortage as demand increases.

To understand how Bitcoin retains value, we must compare the digital currency to gold. The essence of why gold has maintained its value since the Chalcolithic and Bronze Age is due to the precious metal being limited and extraction is challenging. Since fiat money is not pegged to gold anymore after the Gold Standard was abolished, central banks can keep printing money out of thin air which ultimately devalues the currency within a country. Contrastingly, this could never happen to Bitcoin due to the limited and capped supply of 21 million coins. To showcase the various traits of money between gold, fiat (dollar) and crypto (Bitcoin), Sabrina Jiang from Investopedia made the table below to put the comparison into perspective.

Traits of Money	Gold	Fiat (Dollar)	Crypto (Bitcoin)
Fungible (Interchangeable)	High	High	High
Non-Consumable	High	High	High
Portability	Moderate	High	High
Durable	High	Moderate	High
Highly Divisible	Moderate	Moderate	High
Secure (Cannot be counterfeited)	Moderate	Moderate	High
Easily Transactable	Low	High	High
Scarce (Predictable supply)	Moderate	Low	High
Sovereign (Government Issued)	Low	High	Low
Decentralized	Low	Low	High
Smart (Programable)	Low	Low	High

The table above showcases how Bitcoin outshines the traditional gold and fiat traits that have been put on a pedestal throughout history. Gold has always been a favourable investment due to the commodity being a great hedge against inflation, but with the evolution of Bitcoin and certain cryptocurrencies, a more trusted, secure, transferable, profitable and valuable asset now outperforms the traits of gold and fiat by a landslide. Although gold has been quite stagnant, the downfall of Bitcoin is the fact that price fluctuations are volatile due to supply and demand. Even though the market is volatile, the scarcity element of Bitcoin and certain cryptocurrencies is an alluring attraction since this particular manipulation has proven to be a problem in the past in regard to silver.

A perfect example of investors lacking trust within the stock market was in early 2021 when retail investors were trying to coordinate a silver squeeze to prove the discrepancies between reported physical and paper silver figures. This drove retail investors into an ambitious buying frenzy to get their hands on as much physical silver as possible as investors felt deceived by hedge funds and banks. This lack of trust wouldn't happen with Bitcoin and cryptocurrencies that have a capped supply since the capped amount will always be public knowledge through a trusted system based on advanced mathematics.

The difference to buying Bitcoin rather than a stock on the stock market is that with Bitcoin, you are investing in a network of digital currency (digital gold), whereas with stocks you are investing in a corporation. There are no balance sheets or quarterly reports issued for Bitcoin as it is easily accessible for stocks. Instead, technical analysis from charts and the factors of supply and demand (like other commodities) is used to make speculative investment calls. However, one key event that has successfully helped investors determine their Bitcoin investment strategy is based on Bitcoins' infamous "Block Halving Event".

When Satoshi Nakamoto created Bitcoin, there was a rule implemented within the protocol; the rewards miners received for approving transactions would get cut in half every 10,000 blocks, which is every 4 years. When Bitcoin first started in 2009, miners were rewarded with a shocking 50 BTC per block. To put that into perspective, 50 BTC would be worth around $2,500,000 in early 2021. However, 4 years later in 2012, the block rewards got cut to 25 BTC and in 2016 down to 12.5 BTC. This brings us to the recent halving event that just passed in May 2020 where miners are now rewarded 6.25 BTC for every block created. Why is this significant? Simply due to the foundation of Bitcoin being balanced by the supply and demand of the coins in order to maintain value.

From Bitcoin's inception in 2009 to 2020, technical analysis has showcased a consistent pattern of an upward trend on a long-term basis. With the halving event happening every 4 years, the same patterns leading to and following the event has luckily allowed investors to have a clear vision for how the market swayed. There wasn't any significant price increase the day of the event, but the fireworks happened a year later when Bitcoin historically reached a new all-time high price. What goes up must come down, which roughly a year or so after hitting an all-time high, an expected bear (declining) market occurred to correct the market where the price kept plummeting for around a year. After the bear market, the momentum of the market started to pick back up 3 years later - roughly a year before the next halving event. This led the year up to the halving event as a good accumulation phase to start the cycle all over again.

The outline below was created by Eduardo Ricou in his Storm Gain article titled, *Bitcoin Halving Dates History*, that showcased the price action surrounding the halving.

First Halving Event

Date: November 28th, 2012

BTC price at the start: $12

BTC price 100 days later: $42

BTC price 1 year later: $964

Second Halving Event

Date: July 9th 2016

BTC price at the start: $663

BTC price 100 days later: $609

BTC price 1 year later: $2550

Third Halving Event

Date: May 11th 2020

BTC price at the start: $8740

BTC price 100 days later: $11,950

BTC price 11 months later: $60,000

Although there is a growing interest in Bitcoin, there is a lot of controversy stemming from the mainstream media that claims Bitcoin is bogus. Warren Buffet, Donald Trump and Shark Tanks' Kevin O'Leary are amongst the many public figures who have all expressed a deep animosity for Bitcoin, declaring the asset as invaluable. In 2019, Donald Trump went on a Twitter rampage by tweeting, "I am not a fan of Bitcoin and other Cryptocurrencies, which are not money, and whose value is highly volatile and based on thin air." Saying Bitcoin is "based on thin air" clearly showcases his lack of knowledge for the digital currency and the foundation of how money is constructed. If we were to discuss a currency that was based on thin air, let me introduce you to the American dollar.

Since the coronavirus pandemic alone, the federal reserve put trillions of dollars in circulation into the economy, with subtle warnings that more may be added when Biden became president in 2021. Bitcoin is literally generated by cutting-edge mathematics based on supply and demand with the inability to cause inflation. What is the American dollar based on? Thin air.

To add fuel to the fire, in May of 2020, Goldman Sachs held a conference call for their clients to proclaim, "Bitcoin is not a viable investment for client portfolios." The poorly constructed 45 slide presentation that could have been executed in a more informative manner by a 12-year-old, touched base on five points of why "Cryptocurrencies Including Bitcoin Are Not an Asset Class," which are listed below:

- *Do not generate cash flow like bonds.*

- *Do not generate any earnings through exposure to global economic growth.*

- *Do not provide consistent diversification benefits given their unstable correlations.*

- *Do not dampen volatility given the historical volatility of 76% - On March 12, 2020, the price of bitcoin fell 37% in one day.*

- *Do not show evidence of hedging inflation.*

The irrelevant statements their team mentioned above, are as if they took the DeLorean and travelled back in time to the inception of Bitcoin when these questions were initially a concern. Fast forward to 2021 and all of these points have already been debunked. First of all, if Bitcoin is not an asset, then why do we have to pay taxes for something that is not declared an asset? If it is not an asset, then we shouldn't have to pay taxes on it. Unfortunately, we do because it is regarded as an asset.

Cryptocurrency doesn't generate cash flow like bonds because it is not a bond. The only fact that was correct was that the price of Bitcoin did drop 37% to around $5,000 in March 2020, however, this was also the same week as the bombshell announcement of the COVID-19 lockdowns. To showcase the strength of Bitcoin during the 2020 pandemic, the price bounced back quickly and even skyrocketed to $55,000 a year later. This fact alone proved how Bitcoin was a strong investment to hold during an economic crisis, which also acted as a great hedge against inflation. It is interesting how they deterred away from the fact that oil dropped around the same time as the Goldman Sachs presentation. Did they paint oil in a negative light as they did with Bitcoin? Obviously not - what a double standard. It's also funny how something that is "not an asset" has outperformed all other asset classes for the past ten years, but of course, Goldman Sachs keeps quiet about that point.

The final point made on the same slide stated, "We believe that a security whose appreciation is primarily dependent on whether someone else is willing to pay a higher price for it is not a suitable investment for our clients." I'm sorry but that's a load of horse shit right there as this very concept applies to property, stocks and bonds. That is the very reason why people make these investments in the first place, you know...in hopes of gaining a higher return. Common Goldman Sucks, I mean, Goldman Sachs, you can do better than that.

As a result, from the preposterous Goldman Sachs presentation, the billionaire Winklevoss twins who notoriously sued Mark Zuckerberg for stealing their concept for Facebook, did not shy away from voicing their opinions in a few humorous tweets. Cameron Winklevoss stated, "Bitcoin was declared a commodity by the CFTC in 2015 in the coinflip order...so yea it's an asset whose price is set by supply and demand. Just like gold. Just like oil. It's a commodity." Tag teaming on the Goldman Sachs bashing, Tyler Winklevoss joined his brother by tweeting:

"Goldman Sachs: In 2019, $2.8 billion in Bitcoin was sent to currency exchanges from criminal entities.

Fun Fact: Goldman Sachs facilitated $6 billion in money laundering via the 1MDB (Malaysia Development Berhad) scandal between 2012-13.

Double standard much?"

Another notable tweet that flooded Twitter after Goldman Sachs' foolish claims on Bitcoin, was from Ivan On Tech stating, "Hotels hate Airbnb, taxi drivers hate Uber, Nokia hates Apple and banks hate Bitcoin. Losers hate winners." Nailed it.

At the end of the day, negative backlash on Bitcoin is expected due to the currency going against everything that governments and central banks stand for. Due to the pedestal that Goldman Sachs is put on, they are maliciously trying to change the narrative and instil fear into their rich clients for their own benefit. Bitcoin pushes the masses to have control of their own money, so why would those in power want to support such an asset? The positive outcome of this call is that it insinuates the vast interest of Bitcoin from their rich clients so much that a presentation had to be made. Consequently, what are you going to trust – the people who have the ability to lie to make a profit or an advanced mathematical algorithm that has proven to be viable? You be the judge.

Alt Coins

Although Bitcoin is the dominant coin in the sector, there is a vast menu of cryptocurrencies other than Bitcoin that is now classified as alternative coins, which is more commonly known as, "alt coins". The next few pages will discuss the most popular cryptocurrencies in the sector.

Ethereum (ETH)

Ethereum is currently the second largest cryptocurrency based on market capitalisation. The Canadian-based blockchain technology was introduced in 2014 by Vitalik Buterin, who is essentially the modern-day Nikola Tesla of the cryptosphere. While I was blackout drunk making poor life decisions at 19, Buterin ambitiously started to build his proposal for Ethereum. By analysing the main premises of Bitcoin, Buterin based the foundation of Ethereum on a few of the strong points Bitcoin offered but created a handful of extra perks that Bitcoin cannot do.

The best way to imagine Ethereum is to picture it as the internet 2.0, but in a decentralised manner where people can build or use decentralised applications (DApps). Similar to opening the app store on your phone for instance, you can see a selection of applications to choose from within different categories: finance, gaming, technology, arts and collectibles.

Just how we casually go on various websites, the same concept applies to Ethereum, but built specifically where there is no control from an authority to manage. YouTube for instance, is centralised because there is a team of developers behind the scenes controlling the information being shown on the site. The essence of these decentralised applications is to take out the middleman so there is no interference or manipulation with the applications. The applications are run purely based on the coding initially set in stone by the developers, with exception to minor tweakages to fix bugs and updates.

The innovative tech behind Ethereum is due to its initial foundation claiming to be the "new era of the internet", where the below points are stated on the main website to showcase their goals:

- *An internet where money and payments are built in.*

- *An internet where users can own their data, and your apps don't spy and steal from you.*

• *An internet where everyone has access to an open financial system.*

• *An internet built on neutral, open-access infrastructure, controlled by no company or person.*

Although Ethereum is more of a platform rather than a currency or store of value like Bitcoin, the system still has its own cryptocurrency called Ether (ETH), which people can use on the network and profit by trading on exchanges. A huge advantage that Ethereum has over Bitcoin is through its programmable language of decentralised finance (DeFi) by the use of "smart contracts". This is a term used to bind an agreement directly from party A to party B, without the need of a legal representative, central authority or an external middleman to be involved for loans, insurance, crowdfunding, betting or derivatives for instance. A sophisticated computer code executes the text-based contract and is stored on a decentralised blockchain powered platform that makes the smart contracts irreversible, transparent and completely traceable. An example could be if you bought a house and had a mortgage agreement through a DeFi platform, a middleman won't be needed so payments and a contract can be made directly. With most DeFi projects within the cryptosphere running on the Ethereum network, it positions Ethereum as a powerhouse and is disrupting financial technology on a global scale. As the DeFi sector continues to expand with innovative projects, there are now decentralised applications where you can gamble, win crypto prizes, create a passive income, have the ability to trade real life assets through crypto, get a crypto loan, sell digital art (NFT) and now one of the most popular buzzwords within the sector, do something called Yield Farming.

Yield Farming is when interest rewards are given to liquidity providers (LP) when investors offer to lend or exchange their crypto in order for others to borrow, which in some cases for a set period of time. With a smart contract-based liquidity pool, various cryptocurrencies can be locked up depending on which pool is chosen that also showcases the interest that can be earned before locking up crypto. These figures are expressed as a percentage of annual yield (APY). When more investors contribute funds to the associated liquidity pool, the returns of the value increases. Using platforms like Compound or Aave, have gained a lot of attention for either borrowing or loaning cryptocurrencies with interest as high as 37%. The amount of interest made within different Yield Farming pools is quite laughable when comparing the interest rates to traditional banks' lousy return of less than 1%.

The highest interest rate I have seen to date has been an astonishing 600%, but the particular price of the crypto involved (Dogecoin) to lend was extremely volatile. This positioned the lending investment as an extremely risky move since Dogecoin is a joke coin, but if someone was lucky enough to time the market effectively, then a 600% return would be very impressive. All in all, the high interest rates are one of the many reasons why the popularity of Yield Farming was the biggest hit within the DeFi sector in 2020 which spiked from a market cap of $500 million to $10 billion and is expected to keep on growing from here on out.

A new digital craze that has evolved the art collection sector is called Non-Fungible Tokens (NFT). Bitcoin is fungible since we can trade 1 Bitcoin for another Bitcoin that is exactly the same, whereas a non-fungible item is a one-of-a-kind asset. Within this digital avenue, NFTs are powered on Ethereum's blockchain to target the artistic crowd to collect and sell art, music or any creative outlet in a digital format. The best way to imagine an NFT is either a gif, meme, video, music or image that people pay crypto for via ETH. Due to the blockchain element of an NFT, there is a database of owners that is linked to the piece of art to verify how rare the piece actually is. The less the owners, the more the piece is worth. The mind-boggling fact of this new trend is that people have been paying between $1,000 - $1,000,000 just for a digital image, but art is subjective so to each their own.

If you're a creative person who produces any art that is in a digital format, I'd highly recommend looking into selling your work as an NFT as it's a fantastic side hustle, a great way to expand your network and ultimately a unique way to share and express your craft. Although a 5-digit price tag could seem out of reach, I've seen a lot of beginners get between $50-$2000 worth of ETH for their first pieces of NFTs sold. If this interests you, then the below list of sites are currently the best sources to get started within the NFT craze.

- Rarible.com
- Opensea.io
- Superrare.co
- Makersplace.com
- Niftygateway.com

For those of you who enjoy gambling or entering lotteries, then PoolTogether is a protocol constructed on the well-established principle of "no loss lotteries" and "prize savings accounts" that provide an opportunity to win prizes in return for funds being deposited. The interest that accumulates on all user deposits forms the prizes and you also get to keep all of the deposited funds even if you don't win. Another alluring appeal to DeFi is Synthetix which is a token trading platform built on Ethereum that allows users to bet on real world assets – stocks, shares, currencies, precious metals and other assets by using cryptocurrency. As you can hopefully gauge, there is quite an array of options within DeFi to make some extra crypto besides just buying and selling on exchanges. When the crypto market becomes boring, this is when the attention to DeFi becomes popular as it is about taking idle assets and making them into cash positive assets.

Although DeFi is exciting with exceptionally high returns, please bear in mind that this sector is still extremely risky, so it is highly recommended to do more due diligence before diving right in. For further information that pertains to the DeFi sector, defipulse.com acts as the 'leaderboard' for DeFi

as an up-to-date source to gage analytics, informative links for beginners
and rankings of the various DeFi protocols. If DeFi piques your interests,
then it's recommended to check out one of the directory links on the main
webpage that contains an in-depth list for the various platforms connected to
lending, trading, payments, wallets, interfaces, infrastructure, assets scaling,
analytics, education, podcasts, newsletters and even supportive communities
via defipulse.com/defi-list.

In terms of Ethereum's price action, ETH continues to be a leading player
within the crypto space, but it is important to note that ETHs' inception came
six years after Bitcoin. As dominant and high of a price as Bitcoin is, it is
simply due to its long running existence within the market, so alt coins need
time to catch up. My favourite Macro Investor, Raoul Pal, issues informative
newsletters, reports, videos and interviews on his site Real Vision, in which
one of his January 2020 reports claimed that "in terms of market cap, the
virality of ETH is far superior to BTC." He explained that this may be of
surprise to some but it's a fundamental reason as to why he believes that
"ETH has the potential to have a larger market cap than BTC, over time." To
dive into this analysis further, he compared the "network effects" between
the two cryptos to be interestingly similar. "For this we took the starting
point at 1 million active addresses for both, and they are the EXACT same
chart in price and shape, just four years apart."

Exponential assets are hard to determine price targets, however, Raoul Pal
has publicly stated in an interview on the Unchained podcast and within his
Real Vision reports, that his conservative yet bullish target for ETH to hit
within the 2021 bull run is $20,000, which is currently sitting at a $2000
price tag at the beginning of 2021. As shocking as that target is, he sensibly
explains that due to the similar trajectory to Bitcoin, this speculatively
positions this target as a 16x level that BTC was able to hit in the 2017 cycle
from where ETH is sitting in January 2021. "It is the SAME as Bitcoin, at
the same point in its adoption cycle, with the exact SAME price and its
market cap is rising faster... and suggests that its adoption cycle might be

more dramatic too." If ETH follows the same pattern as BTC, then this would allow ETH to outperform BTC within the 2021 bull run and even in the following footsteps of Bitcoin's upward trend within the next few years.

Moving forward, one of the few problems that Ethereum faces is its excruciating high gas fees, slow scalability, speed and security. Many investors have expressed their rage over the high fees on social media to complain that it cost them $50 to convert $100 ETH. However, ETH 2.0 is looming in the distant future in hopes of targeting these issues. Regardless of the negative backlash of Ethereum's high fees, Microsoft announced towards the end of 2020 that the company plans to adopt Ethereum's blockchain to manage gaming royalties, while Reddit announced its first blockchain partnership early 2021 with Ethereum as well. A lot of Ethereum's adoption keeps propelling a bullish case for the cryptos future, however, a big threat to Ethereum is lurking in the distance and that threat is called Cardano.

Cardano (ADA)

If Ethereum is intriguing to you then another crypto that would be good to look into is Cardano (ADA), which is brought forth by the company IOHK. Many crypto fanatics have googly eyes over Cardano since it has been deemed the "Ethereum killer", simply due to its aim to do everything Ethereum can do but better, simpler and with lower transaction costs.

Ironically, Cardano was introduced by one of Ethereum's very own co-founders, Charles Hoskinson and has been one of the fastest growing cryptos to hit the top 5 cryptos on the market. This is due to its peer-reviewed decentralised blockchain platform that is designed to protect user data by incorporating smart contracts and its distributed ledger technology. Although it is still in the early days for Cardano by only being around since September 2017, Cardano claims to be the 3rd generation of cryptocurrency.

The 1st generation was Bitcoin (digital gold), and the 2nd generation is

Ethereum (smart contracts), which both have scaling issues. Cardano takes the previous two generations and combines the two generations to build upon the strengths of the blockchains, but also tackles the weaknesses faced by the first two generations. The three weaknesses that Cardano confidently has set out to solve from the first two generations are sustainability, scalability and interoperability.

Charles regularly discusses the crypto ecosystem when he engages with investors on his live YouTube Q&A, which has gained him a credible appeal from the crypto community due to his insightful, relatable and approachable nature. His ambition behind Cardano is also alluring since he genuinely seems like a good egg just trying to make a difference within a corrupt system. With a bold statement like the one below, it's hard to not like the guy.

> *"Within 5 to 10 years, banks will become less and less relevant, just like landline telephones will be less and less relevant. We're going to wake up one day and be changed by our own money. Jamie Dimon in retirement can watch the world as is and not as the world as he liked it to be."*

In regard to the Cardano vs. Ethereum battle that lies ahead, Hoskinson has been quite vocal with his confidence that Cardano will outperform Ethereum 2.0 within the DeFi sector. Hoskinson co-founded Ethereum by knowing the strengths, challenges, opportunities and threats Ethereum faced, which contrastingly positions Cardano to build a more transparent and efficient network. As exciting as this is to hear, the biggest challenge that Cardano has ahead is its scalability since Ethereum is already the key player within the DeFi ecosystem. Ethereum is years ahead with its trusted network by already having the majority of DeFi projects built onto its blockchain, however, the extremely high gas fees many have been complaining about set Cardano up perfectly since Hoskinson stated that this was a key issue that Cardano will address.

Up until early 2021, Cardano was extremely risky to invest in since it didn't have many advancements or partnerships announced by still being in its testing phases. However, 2021 may just be the year to position Cardano as a major player within the space by slipping into interviews that a government contract with Africa is in its final stages of negotiation. Charles described that "the world is going through an upgrade from a split system to a unified system," since there is a contrast of structure within developed and developing countries where it is reported that roughly 1.7 billion people in developing countries do not have access to a secure financial system.

Those who live in a developed country truly take for granted the accessibility of having a dependable bank account, while the ability to manage finances and have a secure system can be out of reach for those in developing countries. Africa is a hotspot where the continent desperately needs a FinTech revolution and IOHK is specifically targeting the continent where no other crypto organisation has *significantly* made any advancements thus far.

John O'Connor who is the Director of African Operations at IOHK, stated in an interview with Proof of Africa that a partnership "has the potential to be the largest real-world blockchain deployment in the world." The contract alone can wheel in millions of unbanked users onto the Cardano network since Africa is an untouched continent when it comes to blockchain utilisation to solve the many issues at hand. An article published in Crypto Slate mentioned that IOHK also has their eye set on creating partnerships with South Africa, Kenya, Nigeria, Tanzania, and Ethiopia, in addition to adding another 15 countries that will be targeted down the line. This is exciting to read, however, I believe a challenge that IOHK will face is that the Central Bank of Nigeria recently ordered all banks to restrict crypto exchange services within the country. With this in mind, the ability to trade crypto could be limited, but it's not clear as to the governments' stance on using blockchain technology to help citizens with financial services.

Another country that has a negative view on crypto has been India, but it's quite laughable how the regulations have been set in regard to crypto since it keeps changing. One minute crypto is banned and another minute the ban has been revoked, so you can never really gauge the outcome when regulations start to settle in. It will be interesting to see if any developments can flourish within countries that have set a negative outlook on crypto since it loses millions for the economy, which would obviously be a bad move. Hopefully whoever locks in the deal for IOHK is a brilliant negotiator because it would be a home run if Cardano can sign a deal with the Nigerian government in 2021.

Although it has taken longer than expected for Cardano's launch, Hoskinson mentioned in an interview with crypto YouTuber BitBoy Crypto that it was deliberately done to not rush into and fix problems as they went along. Hoskinson explained that they preferred to take their time to fully create a flawless blockchain from the get-go rather than winging it. The fact that Cardano hasn't even launched yet in the beginning of 2021 and IOHK has already announced a mammoth of a potential partnership with a government that will bring in millions, signifies a bold power move that exuberates confidence to set the bar high. They could have focused on smaller partnerships with the launch to get the ball rolling but no, they went all in right away which is confidently daring.

Lastly, to add onto the bullish news for Cardano, there is also speculation that it will be added to the exchange Coinbase within 2021, which would bring in more liquidity. With ADA making its way into the top 5 cryptos by market cap size, potentially processing Africa's finances and above all being named Ethereum's Killer, it is gearing Cardano up on a silver platter for crypto fanatics to feast on. From here on out there are two paths in which IOHK is faced with. Cardano's tech could very well prove its superiority to Ethereum in the coming years and there could be a huge flock to Cardano or, knock on wood, Cardano could flop harder than the movie Cats did on its debut with a shocking 2.8/10 rating. I'd go with the first option as I'm personally rooting for this sleeping giant and really hope that IOHK can prove that they can not only talk the talk, but also walk the walk.

Ripple (XRP)

Due to the barbaric ways of being able to send money internationally, it is quicker to send a text or email than it is to move value across borders. In an age of technological growth, the financial industry is seriously lagging behind. The good news is that now with the introduction of certain cryptocurrencies, this outdated issue is finally being addressed. This is where Ripple comes into the picture to introduce a cutting-edge distributed ledger and blockchain technology to connect liquidity providers, financial institutions and banks with real-time messaging, clearing and settlements of financial transactions. The CTO of Ripple, David Schwartz, perfectly described a scenario of its use in layman's terms on his Quora account:

> *"When you use a credit card to pay for a meal, the restaurant considers you to have paid them and you consider yourself to have paid them, but no money has moved. Really all that's happened is that you now owe some bank money and some bank owes the restaurant money. The bank still has to transfer money to the restaurant's bank account and you still have to pay your credit card bill. The actual movement of money is called 'settlement'."*

Ripple basically took two key fundamentals from Bitcoin, its decentralised speed and cost cutting nature, to raise the stakes by creating a technology that uses a digital currency called XRP as a bridged currency used for settlements on a public ledger. Although Bitcoin is regarded as a store of value now, Ripple's innovative technology is faster, cheaper and more energy efficient than any other cryptocurrency on the market. Bitcoin, for instance, takes 10 minutes to over an hour to complete one transaction and can cost a few dollars to send, whereas using XRP takes 4 seconds and costs a fraction of a penny (0.0001). This structures XRP to be more scalable than Bitcoin to settle payments and why institutions are in awe of Ripple's innovative financial technology.

It is important to note that although you can buy XRP on the market, it is not meant for everyday consumers to go on Amazon and pay for an automated cat feeder for instance. Ripple's network is intended for a backend use case as a bridged currency used for settlements and cross border payments. In other words, you can go to pay for an automated cat feeder on Amazon using American dollars, but on a backend perspective, your fiat money would be converted to XRP as a bridge currency to settle payments behind the scenes. XRP is more comparable to digital gold than an everyday currency for spending, so just how you wouldn't pay for items on Amazon with gold, it's a similar concept when it comes to XRP's utility as a digital asset.

In terms of some of the exciting plans in motion to look forward to in the coming years, Ripple is at the centre of attention within the financial services and banking industry. A pivotal date to keep on your radar is November 22, 2022, where the European Central Bank spearheads the "Big Bang Migration" (ISO 20022) event alongside SWIFT and JP Morgan, in addition to cryptos such as Stellar Lumen (XLM), XinFin (XDC), Algorand (ALGO) and Ripple (XRP). On this date, central banks and communities will simultaneously discontinue the current (older) system and switch to a newer and more innovative system to shift the utilisation of how cross border payments will be made in real time. This migration is single handedly one of the biggest pieces of the puzzle as we shift into a new quantum financial system during this decade.

This news alone simply proves how Ripple is a part of revolutionising the banking industry and they predict that 90% of the world's monetary transactions will be utilising the new ISO 20022 standard by 2023. This is remarkable because there is a flow of 5 trillion dollars of transactions for remittances per day, which means that this alone could easily catapult the price of XRP over $100. For this reason, I strongly believe that the cryptos that are ISO 20022 compliant will be one of the greatest investments of the century. The crypto sector basically pulled a Kanye West while Bitcoin was in the limelight and said, "Imma let you finish Bitcoin, but XRP has the best financial technology of all time." Silly comparison, but if you're too young or too old to get the reference then we'll forget I even said that. If not, hopefully you get the point that no other crypto compares to the utility that XRP has on a global scale.

You're probably thinking that all of this sounds great but what's the catch? Although many institutional buyers and diehard XRP fans view Ripple as a game changer within FinTech, there are many retail investors who loathe the fact that Ripple is out to help the bad guys – the banks and the powers that be. Their mindset is fixated on the fact that the cryptocurrency sector was built upon the foundation of cutting out centralised institutions, yet here Ripple goes hopping into bed with the International Monetary Fund (IMF), European Central Banks, Federal Reserve, SBI Holdings, Saudi Arabia's Central Bank, Santander, American Express, Royal Bank of Canada, Bank of America, Amazon and over 300 other international customers. *Que dramatic music* What a villain! Unpopular opinion, but I believe with more regulations making its way into the sector, cryptos that help the bad guys will be far more superior than those that try to rebel.

Unlike Bitcoin, XRP uses a distributed consensus ledger with a network of validating servers where miners are not needed due to all the coins being already created. The biggest misconception when it comes to XRP is that since Ripple owns the largest amount of XRP, skeptical retail investors interpret that as a way for the company to manipulate the price whenever they please. CEO Brad Garlinghouse addressed this concern on CNN, with anchor Julia Chatterley explaining that the accusation is not in the company's best interest to build a successful ecosystem. Garlinghouse put the debate to rest by stating, "in fact, we have actually taken steps to lock up most of the XRP we own in escrow so we can't touch it."

To continue debunking a lot of the common misconceptions when it comes to

XRP is the site fudbingo.com. This fun site puts together the most common myths that XRP haters try to negatively spin online and debunks the theories by providing links to prove the inaccuracy. For a company that publicly aims to be the Amazon of the crypto sector by 2025, there has been a few hurdles along the way to claiming that dominating title. The biggest curveball to date has come while writing this book with the Securities and Exchange Commission (SEC) slapping a preposterous lawsuit against Ripple in December 2020. After the lawsuit hit, CEO Brad Garlinghouse stated that this lawsuit is not just an attack on Ripple, but the crypto industry as a whole. I personally believe that it is a bit ridiculous that Ripple has been working closely with U.S. regulators for over 7 years and then the SEC turns around and hits this lawsuit on one of the most credible companies within the industry.

The main premise of the lawsuit is that the SEC alleged that XRP is an unregistered security and Ripple's sales of it within the early days of its inception were illegal since they deem XRP as a *security* and not a *currency*. The SEC is alleging that retail investors who purchased XRP feel that they also own 'shares' of Ripple the company, which would classify it as a security. However, the negative backlash from retail investors showcases that the majority are actually well aware they're investing in a currency like a commodity, rather than investing into Ripple the company.

To stir the pot even more a few days after the SEC filed a lawsuit against Ripple, the crypto exchange Coinbase also got hit with a lawsuit since the platform sold XRP as an 'unregistered security' to retail investors. It's a bit odd that not all exchanges within the sector also got hit with the same lawsuit, but that's just one of the many flaws within all of the chaos. What's comical though is now Coinbase has to prove within their own lawsuit how XRP is indeed a currency instead of a security, which will help Ripple's case. To add a bit more spice to the pot, investors of XRP were outraged by the outrageous lawsuit against Ripple that caused XRP to drop over 66%, that a class action lawsuit was filed against the SEC spearheaded by a lawyer (@JohnEDeaton1) who invests in XRP.

This class action lawsuit is suing on the grounds of market manipulation and to deem XRP as a currency as investors were not misled by Ripple's marketing that they own shares or dividends within the company. It is the SEC's duty to protect investors' best interests and by filing this ludicrous lawsuit against Ripple, they failed miserably by claiming that XRP is a security. What is even more laughable is the fact that one of Ripple's attorneys, Stuart Alderoty, stated in 2020 that the SEC used Ripple's tech without authorisation. To be honest, the whole legal situation at the beginning of 2021 is like watching an episode of Suits. Plus, the cherry on top of all of this is that one of Ripple's attorneys used to work directly for the SEC. Former Chair of the SEC Mary Jo White, has also chimed in and publicly stated that, "there's no way to sugarcoat it. The SEC is dead wrong legally and factually." Good old irony – we love to see it.

In a YouTube video with crypto influencer and Journalist Layah Heilpern, she interviewed Michael Arrington, who is the Venture Capitalist and Founder of TechCrunch and Arrington XRP Capital, to pick his brain about the SEC vs. Ripple lawsuit. "The SEC is an entity that changes over time and is changing right now in terms of SEC chairs. What the SEC chair wants over time is largely dependent on what the executive branch wants." When Leah asked his views of what XRP should be classified as, he stated, "do I think it's a security from the point of view of the SEC? No, but from my point of view, it doesn't matter. What is a security and what isn't a security is irreverent and it really comes down to if you only allow rich people to trade an asset or if you allow everybody to trade an asset?" He went on to say that he had the advantage of investing in the first rounds of Uber, Pinterest and Airbnb simply because he had wealth and owned a venture fund. He explained that "everyday people" that could be smarter than him also wanted to invest, but couldn't because the government told them that they're not worthy enough. They couldn't make proper decisions for themselves, so they weren't allowed to invest during the first rounds to make 10,000x returns.

"The same damn thing is happening where the SEC comes in and says we don't want poor people, their definition of poor, to make decisions that rich people are, so we'll stop them from doing that. That's evil! So, who cares what the definition of what a security is at the end of the day?"

A domino effect that followed the lawsuit is that a handful of exchanges delisted or suspended trading of XRP while the case still carries on. In addition, the media has spread fear that XRP is a dead-end coin and that retail investors should steer clear, which interestingly enough, the same mainstream narrative happened within the early days of the dotcom bubble. Many moons ago when the sound of dial up internet gave the same reaction as nails on a chalkboard, the media was publicly stating that retail investors should not invest in AOL, Dell and Microsoft since they publicly claimed that the internet won't last. Let's just take a moment to laugh at the negative remarks of people and publications who stated that the internet won't last.

On a serious note, right after the widespread fear to shake out the retail investors from investing in internet stocks and for institutions to get cheap prices, 1995-2000 saw a massive bull market (when the market is in an uptrend) where 5 trillion dollars flooded the market specifically because of the rise of internet stocks. The upsetting part of all of this is that manipulating the news cycle is irrationally not illegal because it benefits the powers that be, rather than the underdogs. While keeping this in mind, I strongly feel that history will repeat itself and is painting XRP within the same negative scenario due to its ground-breaking utility and functionality on a global scale.

An insightful interview that discusses the manipulation within the markets is a YouTube video with investing mogul Teeka Tiwari titled, 'Glenn Beck Discusses The Great Bitcoin Cryptocurrency Conspiracy XRP TV HD 2018.' I was enraged after watching the interview to be honest because it easily puts the coerced manipulation into perspective, so out of spite, I bought even more XRP. A lot of times when people say to not do something, it just makes you want to do it even more. Surely, I'm not the only one who thinks this right? XRP is like the big shiny red button that retail investors are told not to touch, but because I don't have much self-control, I push it anyways to see what will happen.

Although it is still early days for the lawsuit beginning in 2021, Ripple's defence team publicly posted their preliminary legal response before their first hearing, which took place on February 22nd, 2021. To help the XRP Community, attorney Jeremy Hogan has been uploading insightful videos to his YouTube channel Legal Briefs, to simply break down the fundamentals of the case to give a legal perspective in layman's terms. After reading Ripple's preliminary legal response, he stated that he was blown away at how strong of a case Ripple has over the SEC. He even described that when he read the Affirmative Consensus section that he felt as if he was "Morpheus in The Matrix." If you have not seen the movie to get the reference, it is insinuating a groundbreaking moment - an 'ah ha' moment if you will.

Hogan explained that the response signified that Ripple is not trying to beat around the bush as plenty of other cases tend to do and is specifically asking for a quick turnaround. He highlighted that Rippled filed a "genius" motion under the Federal Sunshine Law to request documents from the SEC as to why Ethereum is not a security. Ripple stated that Ethereum had an Initial Coin Offering (ICO) which is similar to the stock markets Initial Public Offering (IPO) when a company goes public. Funnily enough, Ripple never had an ICO, but Ethereum did. Hogan also highlighted Ripple's point that Ethereum, back in the day, were "selling securities", so why the proclamation in 2018 by the SEC that Ethereum wasn't deemed as a security? He stated that Ripple demanding for this proof, turned the tables onto the SEC to defend themselves rather than hitting a home run that they expected. Also, the fact that Ripple has an attorney on their side who used to work for the SEC is wonderful because they know very well the ins and outs of how the SEC has conducted business and regulations in the past.

The most exciting part of Hogan's video was his "bombshell moment," in which he explained in Ripple's Affirmative Defense section of the preliminary response, that the SEC didn't sue for a declaratory judgment that XRP was a security. The SEC could have asked for a ruling within the case for the courts to declare if XRP is a security as they have publicly claimed, but they left that part out of the most important section of the filing. They only asked for monetary damages that could also affect the escrow Ripple owns that are locked up. Peculiar if you ask me but as a result, Ripple has personally demanded within their defence for the court to determine the regulatory clarity that they have been desperately seeking ever since the inception of XRP. It is also important to note that Ripple's business is 95% international even though its headquarters is in the US simply due to the lack of regulatory clarity within America.

The frustrating part of Ripple doing business within America is that the US is the only country out of the G20 to not have clear regulations set if XRP is a security or a currency, as all other countries have already deemed it as a digital currency. Funny thing is that in the filing, the SEC claimed that Ripple self-labeled XRP as a currency, but Ripple argued that they have an agreement with the US Financial Crimes Enforcement Network (FinCEN) that the governing bureau labeled XRP as a currency back in 2015. By hearing Hogan say this bombshell, paints the picture that the SEC is simply filing a lawsuit to try and get Ripple to squeeze out a huge lump sum of cash and scare retail investors out of investing before XRP explodes. The worst-case scenario could be that Ripple would have to pay a hefty settlement and may have to give up their XRP in escrow, which some investors believe could be handed over to the International Monetary Fund (IMF) to manage. Another theory floating around is that XRP could be deemed as a 'derivative security', which isn't necessarily a bad call since it would benefit the quadrillion dollar derivatives market. These two outcomes are highly speculative of course, but regardless of the outcome of the lawsuit, I am confident that Ripple will continue to thrive after finally getting regulatory clarity and I believe that's when the fun really begins for early investors.

In regard to a timeline for how long the lawsuit can drag on for, Hogan hinted that the most likely outcome would be for Ripple to settle and this could potentially happen between September 2021-February 2022. Although there could be many curve balls along the way, this is to be taken lightly as an estimated guess based on the timeline of one of his personal cases that lines up with Ripple's lawsuit.

When digging into the SEC's past, I had a sense of déjà vu as two similar situations happened with Tesla and Amazon since the SEC slapped both companies with a securities fraud lawsuit. As you can imagine, the press shoved fear down investors' throats and the stock prices fell until after the lawsuit settled and both stocks skyrocketed months later. The same thing also happened with Crypto Kik Interactive Inc., where the SEC filed a lawsuit in 2019 since they claimed that the company sold its KIN tokens without registering them accordingly by U.S. security laws. KiK settled the lawsuit in October 2020 and right after, the price spiked 40x. I strongly believe that the same price spike will happen when the SEC vs Ripple lawsuit gets tossed out the window since XRP is far more powerful than a crappy crypto such as KiK. To be conservative with numbers, if XRP was to spike 40x from the current listed price of $0.59, that would bring the price to around $23.00. There are also a lot of prospective clients waiting on the side-lines until Ripple gets the regulatory clarity it desperately needs before doing business, so this will also help XRP's price after the lawsuit. With this in mind, I believe a $10-$25 XRP price tag after the lawsuit blows over is quite realistic.

If you're reading this book while the lawsuit is still going on, I'd highly recommend watching attorney Jeremy Hogan's YouTube videos to stay up to date with the case. As daunting as the lawsuit may seem from a first glance, Hogan has honestly been such a saint during these unsettling times and has easily put the XRP community's minds at ease with his entertaining, yet informative videos. A wonderful quote by billionaire tycoon Warren Buffet that has guided me through the treacherous downfall of the lawsuit has been, "be fearful when others are greedy and greedy when others are fearful." There is fear on the streets due to the lawsuit, however, I personally view this downfall as a great buying opportunity to feed off the fear and have been as greedy as I can while the price of XRP is still dirt cheap. Whatever curveballs are thrown along the way, I will still remain in Ripple's corner throughout the case. This is simply due to knowing how powerful Ripple's innovation and partnerships are in addition to knowing the future plans lined up – i.e., ISO 20022. Regardless of whether you invest in Ripple or not, knowing the long-term plans of the cryptos you invest in is essential to allow you to keep your eyes on the prize when the market dips, or in Ripple's case, when lawsuits are thrown into the picture.

To cast a positive light onto XRP for the long-term comes an exciting partnership that has blossomed with the Flare Network (FLR) that should launch June 2021. In layman's terms, Flare integrates with Ethereum's Virtual Machine (EVM) as a bridge between networks to blend Ethereum's strengths of smart contracts, in conjunction with XRP's increased payment speed, reliability of payment and best of all, it's cost-effective fees that are a fraction of a penny. This is a deadly combo for both cryptos to tag team the DeFi sector since 75% of the value existing on blockchain projects are unable to utilise smart contracts. This dynamic partnership gives me dollar-sign eyes as all I can think about is the quadrillion dollar derivatives market. For those who want to see a visual representation of the world's entire wealth and compare how big or small each market is, then I highly recommend looking at the link below that directs to a Venture Capitalist article titled, "All of the World's Money and Markets in One Visualisation". The best comparison of this article is to compare it to the instructional outer space videos floating online that showcases how the size of each planet compares to one another. The link is truly mind boggling to grasp how big the derivatives market truly is.

https://bit.ly/2MF7M4Y

Once you've scraped your jaw off the floor from looking at how dominating the derivatives market truly is in comparison to other markets, it's essential to know what the heck a derivative is. To explain the complex market in layman's terms, imagine someone you know has a limited-edition Star Wars lightsaber that the current value is $5,000, but this person isn't a big enough fan to know its true value. In this example, you'll be a proclaimed Star Wars fanatic in which you're confident that the value of said lightsaber will go up within a year. However, even though you'd like to buy it at the moment, you don't have the funds to offer right away. You bring up the fact that you want to buy the lightsaber in a year to give enough time to save and will offer $8,000 instead. Instantly the original owner is sold on the idea and a contract is created to bind the agreement together that outlines the specifics. Time goes by and some sort of significant Star Wars charade happens that increases the value of the lightsaber to be worth $10,000 a year later. Although the value increased over a year, the underlying terms of the agreement remain valid that you'd still have to pay $8,000 – even if the value dropped below. This principal is the main premise of what the derivatives market is all about – a contract between two or more parties where the value is based on an agreed upon financial asset.

By viewing the link above of the world's wealth, you can visually gauge how vast the derivatives market truly is and how much money would flow through XRP and Flare if they can get a piece of that big pie. Word on the street is that Ripple's end goal is for XRP to manage the *entire* quadrillion dollar derivatives market. If this was to happen, the price of 1 XRP that is currently $0.59, will be a distant memory in the coming years when the price of XRP has the potential to hit 3 or dare I say...even 4 digits.

To try and put these high price targets into perspective from a technical analysis point of view, the YouTube account Working Money Channel uploaded a video titled, "Ripple XRP: If Bitcoin Does This, Could XRP Really Reach +$100/XRP By The Fall Of 2022?" The summary of the video explained that a $100 price point towards the end of 2022 isn't actually as absurd as it sounds. The crypto YouTuber discussed a price target that was initially brought into the light within the Twitter XRP community with a thread made by @XRPPatience, who explained that over the years, the patterns at which the crypto market had an uptrend always lasted longer than the previous upward cycle. For this reason, it is easy to speculate that the same thing may happen again. This could mean that from the beginning of 2021, up until the end of 2022, XRP *could* see a huge price increase within the market, until it falls back down into a bear market (downward trend) for a few years until the next Bitcoin halving event. If this is the case, he explained that basic chart patterns that have happened within the past bull market are lining up again early 2021 to form a similar pattern.

To conclude the thread of tweets, @XRPPatience stated, "Whether you look at XRP from a technical or fundamental aspect, given the likely length of this bull cycle, the growing institutional involvement, XRP's vast and growing net worth and ecosystem makes a $100 XRP not at all unrealistic by fall of 2022." If XRP can actually hit that target in 2022, within 2025 or even 2027, it is important to note that Ripple is not a get rich quick coin. Ripple is literally revolutionising the new world of finance and with that prodigious title comes extreme patience, which makes XRP a long-term hold for the next few years. To conclude, I personally feel that those who have strong hands when it comes to XRP will reap the greatest rewards as investing in XRP for the long-term is a rare opportunity to climb up the ladder of wealth.

Stellar Lumen (XLM)

Although Stellar Lumen (XLM) is not amongst the top 5 coins on coinmarketcap.com at the moment, Stellar has definitely pulled the attention of many investors as a crypto to look out for within the next few years. Stellar has an interesting backstory after Ripple's co-founder Jed McCaleb, branched away from Ripple to similarly create the nonprofit Stellar Development Foundation in 2014 with his ex-girlfriend, Joyce Kim. During the early days, McCaleb wrote an article for Bitcoin magazine and stated:

"Why Stellar? After years of working in the FinTech space, I realised that the world's financial infrastructure is fundamentally broken, leaving billions without resources. As a result, Joyce Kim and I co-founded Stellar.org to create an open standard for financial technology. Since anyone can participate in the network, it can be particularly helpful for the 2 billion unbanked people worldwide."

Unlike Bitcoin that runs on a 'Proof-of-Work' blockchain, XLM doesn't require 'miners' since it's similar to XRP running on a consensus network where all the coins are already created. Instead of having miners approve transactions every 10 minutes, a consensus-based network automatically links servers together to validate. Similar to Bitcoin, the scarcity of Stellar's coins will always have a capped supply of 50 billion coins within the ecosystem. As demand increases for Stellar, the limited supply also helps with XLM's price action.

The live Stellar ecosystem is entirely operated by its community outside of Stellar.org as the network responds to an open-source core protocol. This adds value to the network to make it functional and efficient since the ecosystem is up to the Stellar community. An example of the community coming together was back in September 2020 when members voted to burn (get rid of) half of its initial coin supply. This was a collaborated effort to create a more structured ecosystem in hopes of benefitting future developments. The current supply of 50 billion XLM is now set in stone since the community has also voted to eliminate the inflation of the coin back in October 2019, which has received positive feedback which instantly increased the price by 25% the same day. Stellar has more upside potential now due to its limited supply of coins making the total coins far less than XRP which has 100 billion coins total. Although some investors are fearful with Ripple's lawsuit, since XLM is very similar to Ripple's tech, some investors have hopped ship to invest with XLM to reduce risks within their investments with XRP.

To start 2021 off, Stellar released its 2021 report to highlight that the organisation's main focus is to scale developers, transactions and partnerships and to actively make sure that the network won't be stagnant and to increase public awareness. One of the most exciting pieces of news to kick off 2021 was that Stellar announced their partnership with the Ukrainian government to facilitate its own Central Bank Digital Currency (CBDC) infrastructure using Stellar's FinTech. In addition, the partnership between Circle and Coinbase issued its 'stablecoin' USDC on Stellar's network, which is the second largest stablecoin that is pegged to the American dollar 1:1. With the pressure on for the US to digitise the dollar, since China is currently in the lead by already rolling tests out for the digital Yuan, many crypto fanatics *speculatively* believe that the U.S. will eventually run its own CBDC on Stellar's network.

In addition to focusing on CBCDs, Stellar announced at the beginning of 2021 its plans to build upon its blockchain by prioritising the desire to expand into the decentralised finance (DeFi) sector by integrating smart contracts. The combination of issuing cross border payments within seconds for a fraction of a penny, in conjunction with the ability to lend and borrow funds on its network, could give Ethereum a run for its money within the DeFi sector. Ethereum users have recently been projecting a lot of negative backlash online for the ridiculously high fees at the moment by tweeting complaints that fees have been as high as $350 for buying or sending $50 worth of ETH. Although it is currently problematic to use Ether as a payment method, Ethereum's high fees have been advantageous to put XLM in the spotlight for what is to come. By also landing major partnerships with Deloitte, IBM and Stripe, as well as a dozen financial institutions and payment processors on a global scale, this positions Stellar's network as a favourable leader within the crypto space.

With the rise of digital currencies, central banks are starting to gear towards digitalising fiat and partnering with Stellar would be an easy transition for central banks to do so. However, due to its similar tech to Ripple, many believe that this is where Ripple and Stellar will battle it out for who will come out on top to win the CBDC race. Ripple just hired a new Senior Director at the end of 2020, in which their role will be to specifically focus on locking in deals with central banks to use Ripple's FinTech. Could this be a battle between the two cryptos as to which one will be superior when it comes to tackling CBDCs or will there be a level playing field between Ripple and Stellar to coexist?

Only time will tell, but Stellar Lumen is also one of the few that is part of the anticipated ISO 20022 migration, which again positions Stellar Lumen as a sleeping giant. As a result, let's daydream for a second by doing some speculative calculations. If XLM was successful in being the leading blockchain to run all CBDCs, 100 trillion dollars of the broad money supply within the world could flow through Stellar's network. In Crypto Loves' YouTube video titled, "Stellar Lumen - Could $39 XLM Make You a Millionaire...Realistically???", the crypto influencer forecasted how much gains someone *could...*key word here is *could...* get as a return if Stellar was successful in being the leading blockchain to host CBDCs.

In the last bull market of March 2017, the market capitalisation (how much a company or crypto is worth within a market) for Stellar was $12.4 million, with a price tag of $0.0017 per coin. The price multiplied with a return of 541x to bring the price at the end of January 2018 to an all-time high of $0.92 and a market cap of $16.5 billion before the market dropped back down. If someone invested $1,848 into Stellar back then and held their position from March 2017-January 2018, the return would have hit above a whopping one million dollars. Now, with Stellar positioning its ecosystem to central banks to be the number one host for Central Bank Digital Currencies to run on, it creates a stronger case for Stellar to have a brighter future and effectively go beyond its previous all-time high price. To try and speculate how much an investor would have to invest to make a million dollars within a new up-trending cycle, Crypto Love used the same growth calculations within the last bull run to chart future price predictions if someone was to invest

41

$1000 into Stellar this time around.

The video was originally published in December 2020 where the price for one XLM was $0.17 with a market cap of 3.9 billion, so if $1000 was invested into XLM with the price of $0.17, this would equal to owning 5,882 XLM. Based on the previous growth metrics to hit its previous all-time high market cap of 16.5 billion, the price would equate to $0.71 with a gain of $4176.22. Although profit would be made, it's still nowhere near a million dollars as before. However, with all the institutional and retail interest that the market has gained in comparison to when Stellar previously hit its all-time high price, Crypto Love made further calculations to see how long it would take for a $1000 investment in Stellar to turn into a million dollars if someone invested late 2020 or early 2021. The chart below outlines a play-off of his calculations using the same metrics until the market cap hits 100 trillion, which takes into consideration the 100 trillion of broad money on a global basis.

Investment	XLM	Market Cap	Price	Gains
$1000	5882	16.5 Billion	$0.71	$4176.22
$1000	5882	176 Billion	$7.64	$44,938.48
$1000	5882	5 Trillion	$217.22	$1,277,688.04
$1000	5882	100 Trillion	$4,344.49	$25,554,290.18

To put market caps into perspective, below are the top S&P 500 companies to truly grasp how vast a 100 trillion-dollar market cap actually is.

- Bitcoin - 1 T
- Apple - 2.30 T

- Microsoft - 1.83 T
- Amazon - 1.67 T

To reference back to the Visual Capitalist article a few pages back, the article visually showcases the world's wealth to grasp how ridiculously high a 100 trillion-dollar market cap truly is – especially since the whole crypto market literally just hit 1 trillion collectively in the beginning of 2021. Below is the link again for ease of reference.

https://bit.ly/2MF7M4Y

At first it may seem unattainable and quite laughable, however, comparing the top S&P 500 companies is a lot different than if a particular blockchain network is processing the total value of the world's entire money supply. This includes coins, banknotes, money market accounts, savings, checking and time deposits. Latching onto this big piece of pie *could* very well catapult Stellar's market cap (if successful) to scratch the surface of dare we say...the trillions. Is a trillion-dollar market cap possible? Yes. Could it happen with Stellar? Potentially. This is strictly due to its real-life utility that still makes it undervalued. Now the question is, will this actually happen? Who bloody knows, but Stellar has the firepower to make it possible – especially because of ISO 20022. This is all speculation of course, but if investors are willing to sit on a long-term investment within XLM with the end goal of a trillion dollar plus market cap in mind, this *could* very well be one of the greatest tales to ever be told if you were lucky enough to get in early.

Dogecoin

I wasn't going to discuss Dogecoin initially due to the fact that it is a coin based on a joke, but after the Wall Street Bet fiasco in early 2021, I realised that I needed to address the coin since it has received viral attention and has become a new cultural movement. To start off, Dogecoin should not be taken seriously as it is literally based on the meme of a Shiba Inu. There are no fundamentals when it comes to the coin as it pumps and dumps due to social media attention – particularly when Elon Musk tweets about it or when Doge is trending on Twitter. Unlike other cryptocurrencies, you cannot do proper technical analysis or even look at a chart to gage the direction of where the coin is going to go because it is based on social media hype.

It is great that this joke coin has drawn people into the wonderful world of crypto, but it is nerve wracking to see so many people hop on board the Doge train without knowing what they're getting themselves into. It's all fun and games when Elon Musk tweets a funny Doge related image and the price pumps, but a lot of newbies do not know how to collect profits and then all of a sudden, the price comes crashing down which turns smiles into frowns. Doge pumps hard but it also crashes hard as well, so if you do end up investing in Doge, come to terms that it is no different than if you were at a casino gambling with your money.

If you're ok with that then fair play, but if that thought makes you uncomfortable, then Doge is probably not the crypto for you. The pumps are exhilarating if you can ride the wave from the bottom to the top, but if you joined the bandwagon late at the top and then all of a sudden the price comes crashing down hard, the acceptance of loss is a psychological battle that many have had to face and come to terms with. It's called a pump and dump coin for a reason and for that reason, I would personally stay far away.

Alt Coin Summary

Although there are over 5000 different cryptocurrencies within the sector with widely different attributes, the ones mentioned in this chapter are the most popular ones that beginners tend to be drawn to. You can have XLM and ADA for a starter, XRP as the main and have BTC as dessert. Not satisfied enough? Then munch on some ETH on the side. Whatever the combo, it is good to know that there is a vast basket of various cryptocurrencies other than Bitcoin since alt coins are on the rise to outperform the dominant crypto.

A great website to see a full list of other cryptos within the sector, can be found at coinmarketcap.com or livecoinwatch.com which is ranked based on market capitalisation. These sites allows users to dig a bit deeper into each crypto to gage the credibility, size, ranking, basic analytics and some news pertaining to various cryptos. If you hear about a crypto but don't know if it would be a good investment or not, quickly head over to these sites to search the crypto to see its ranking to scope its potential and basic fundamentals. If you are looking for crypto on the site and it does not appear or has a very poor ranking in the thousands, then that would be considered a highly risky investment.

It is also important to note that in the stock market, the S&P 500 tracks the stocks of the largest 500 companies, which investors tend to use as a benchmark to compare the progress of their large cap investments against the market. There isn't an equivalent to S&P 500 in the crypto market, however, since Bitcoin has built such a dominant place within the sector, comparing alt coins performance to Bitcoin's performance is a similar way of tracking progress. On the exchanges where you buy and sell crypto or even on sites such as coinmarketcap.com and tradingview.com, you can view charts that are easy to comprehend to see the performance of your portfolio or other cryptos within the sector and compare it to Bitcoin's performance.

When you do finally take the leap of faith to invest, regardless of whether you invest in Bitcoin or not, it's essential to know that based on historical data, Bitcoin's dominance within the sector moves the market. If Bitcoin goes up, alt coins tend to follow suit and when Bitcoin goes down, alt coins go down as well. A pattern that also happens is when Bitcoin hits an all-time high price or loses dominance, that is usually when profits were taken to then reinvest into alt coins. This is called 'alt season' where the site Blockchain Center explains that, "if 75% of the Top 50 coins performed better than Bitcoin over the last season (90 days) it is Altcoin Season." The link on the next page has a useful Altcoin Season Index that visually showcases bar graphs and lists the top 50 coins to compare the alt coins to Bitcoin's dominance.

https://bit.ly/3eFqqVo

As of 2021, Bitcoin will continue to be the go-to crypto within the sector due to the advantage of being the most popular one. Once people get comfortable with their position within Bitcoin, then that's when attention towards Ethereum grows since it's the runner up within the market. As investors start realising the innovation within the space, the attraction towards other alt coins tend to follow suit. With institutional interest now in the sector after 2020, there is a new wave of interest in contrast to the 2017 bull market since it was predominantly retail investors. This is a huge shift within the market as millions and billions of institutional money aka smart money, will now flow into the sector which never happened in the past…well, that was public knowledge at least. With so many amazing advancements within the various crypto projects and the flood of institutional money, this positions 2021 to be an explosive year, before the market dips back down into a bear market to start accumulating.

Renown Global Macro Investor Raoul Pal stated on his Twitter account that investing in crypto is the "future" and proclaims that investing within the sector is the most exciting investment opportunity he has seen within his whole 30 plus years within the financial industry. "The metaverse, the internet of value, store of value, pristine collateral and an entirely new future is beyond BIG. It is the next and biggest part of the internet revolution and it's only just started." We are in the midst of a digital asset revolution and it will be exciting to see if any cryptos can dethrone Bitcoin to take the primary position within the market. Do I think that's possible in 2021? I don't, but in the coming years, I do believe that is indeed very possible – especially with XRP and XLM lurking in the distance.

Lastly, depending on when you're reading this book, please note that the sector advances very swiftly. I recommend doing further due diligence into the cryptos that pique your interest to keep on top of the news, as what I mentioned in this chapter could be a different outcome to when this book falls into your lap. Hopefully that isn't the case, but it will be a key thing to do before taking the plunge and investing.

3

Crypto Lingo

"The expert at anything was once a beginner."

- Helen Hayes

W hen it comes to learning about the cryptocurrency sector, there is an array of new terminology that beginners stumble upon that can be confusing and this chapter is to introduce the most common terms in a simplified manner. Although there is a vast list of other technical terms and phrases that you will stumble upon along the way of your crypto journey, this chapter lists the common terms and phrases that every beginner should familiarise themselves with before diving into the sector.

All-time high (ATH) - When the price of an asset reaches its highest recorded value.

Example: Many investors believe Bitcoin will reach its previous all-time high of $20,000 before the end of 2020.

All-time low (ATL) - When the price of an asset reaches its lowest recorded value.

Example: Some investors believe that Bitcoin has to reach an all-time low in 2018 before the price can spike after the May 2020 halving event.

Bear Market (Bearish) - A negative term expecting that a price or market will decrease.

Example: I hope the effects of coronavirus doesn't push the sector into a bear market.

Bull Market (Bullish) - A positive term expecting that a price or market will increase.

Example: There's so much bullish news circulating around XRP, I'm excited for the future!

Buy - An investment term used to enter a market to purchase a security, crypto, stock, currency or commodity.

Example: I am going to diversify my portfolio and buy more Bitcoin before 2020 ends because Citibank predicts that it will hit $300,000 by the end of 2021.

Central Bank - A financial institution that operates as a monetary authority and controls the currency, interest rates, and cash supply of a state or formal monetary union.

Circulating Supply - Represents the amount of publicly accessible and circulating cryptocurrency coins and tokens on the market.

Decentralised Exchanges (DEXes) - A peer-to-peer exchange to trade crypto without the need of an institution or company providing the platform.

Digital Wallet - Just how we can have physical wallets, cryptocurrencies have digital wallets that come in various forms. I.e. - paper wallets (not safe if they get destroyed), desktop wallets (not safe from hackers) and the safer option, an offline physical hardware wallet that resembles a USB stick. Chapter 6 will discuss this in greater detail.

Dump/dumping - Dumping is a term used to sell a large portion of your cryptocurrency. Dumping is when a lot of people in the market are selling their position to cause a drastic price drop.

Example: I'm going to dump all my Litecoin and put it into Bitcoin in 2020.

Exchanges - A place where you can conduct fair trade of anything of value. In simple terms, this is where you can buy, send, sell and store your cryptocurrency. The next chapter will discuss the various exchanges in more detail.

Fiat Money - Government issued currency.

Example: USD is the fiat in the United States and GBP is the fiat in the United Kingdom.

FUD - A negative acronym used to create fear, uncertainty and doubt.

Example: CNBC had Kevin O'Leary on the show Squawk Box to create FUD about Bitcoin.

Hold - An investment strategy where investors have placed a buy on a crypto and expect the value to increase over a long period of time to then sell and collect profits at a later date.

HODL - The real meaning of HODL is derived from an investor who drunkenly posted on the forum Bitcointalk in 2013 and made a typo when typing the word "hold" and instead wrote "hodl". It instantly became a viral sensation and the crypto community now refers to the holding of a position as "hodling". A popular alternative meaning is being an acronym for, "hold on for dear life."

Example: I plan on hodling XRP for the next 7 years.

ICO - Short for 'initial coin offering.' An ICO is when an organisation publicly offers their coin to raise money just like crowdfunding. The same concept applies in the stock market but is called an "initial public offering" (IPO) instead. Both offerings are a way for the organisation to raise capital.

Long/Long Position - The anticipation that the value of a crypto will increase in price over a long period of time. If you were to buy and hold XRP for the next few years for instance, this would be a long position since you hope the value goes up over a long period of time.

Market Cap - Short for "market capitalisation" to represent the total market value of a coin. The market cap of a coin is calculated by the below formula:

Market Cap = Circulating Supply x Price

Moon - Positive slang to indicate that the price of a coin will rapidly increase in value - so much that it will be astronomical and skyrocket.

Example: Bitcoin will be mooning in 2021. We're going to the moon!

Private Keys - Think of your private key as your personal password to access your cryptocurrency. Exchanges and wallet companies for instance, will NEVER text, email or call you to say that there are problems with your account. Scammers have used this excuse to claim that people must send their private keys to fix the issue. Don't fall victim to this as your private keys are for your eyes only!

Public/Digital Address - A unique sequence of 27 to 34 letters and numbers used to represent a digital wallet just as a bank account. When someone tries to safely send cryptocurrency, a digital address must be entered before sending.

Example of a digital address: 137std6I9PxxyDjPPLLsMLqDbP6Nxpp8DJ

Public Key - A unique string of letters and numbers that make it easy to receive cryptocurrency. Although the term states that it is public, the unique keys are only made public once the owner has publicly shared their details in order to receive cryptocurrency. It can be used to easily get cash out, however, using a public address has been deemed a safer option.

Pump and Dump - A sneaky tactic some investors do by teaming up with a group of other investors to try and increase the value of a coin. This is done so they can sell when the price increases to quickly sell and collect their profits. Whatever goes up must come down and after the pump, the dump will come.

Beware when public crypto influencers have titles for videos or articles that claim, "3 coins to get rich quick!"

ROI - Short for "return on investment."

Satoshi - A common Bitcoin misconception is that investors have to buy the full price of what Bitcoin is worth at the time of purchase. This is not the case as the smallest unit of Bitcoin is called a Satoshi, which is named as a homage to the creator of Bitcoin - Satoshi Nakamoto. The same concept of buying a fraction of any coin applies to all other cryptocurrencies as well.

1 Bitcoin for example, is equivalent to 100 million satoshi:

1 Satoshi = 0.00000001 BTC
10 Satoshi = 0.0000001 BTC
100 Satoshi = 0.000001 BTC
1000 Satoshi = 0.00001 BTC
10000 Satoshi = 0.0001 BTC
100 000 Satoshi = 0.001 BTC
1 000 000 Satoshi = 0.01 BTC
10 000 000 Satoshi = 0.1 BTC
100 000 000 Satoshi = 1 BTC

Selling - An investment strategy used to exit a position within a market.

Short/Shorting - The opposite of a long position when betting against the market that a crypto will decrease in value.

Stablecoins - A type of cryptocurrency that has its value pegged to another asset. These coins can be linked to fiat currencies such as the dollar of the

United States, other cryptocurrencies, precious metals or a mix of the three. Due to Bitcoin's volatility, supporters claim that stablecoins help remove doubts in regard to exchange rates, which makes these cryptocurrencies more feasible for purchasing products and services. Although stablecoins are still relatively new in the market, it can play a vital role when trying to integrate cryptocurrencies into traditional financial markets.

The Binance exchange for instance, offers two stablecoins that are fiat-backed – BGBP which is pegged to the British Pound and BUSD which is tied to the US dollar. Other stablecoins include Tether (USDT), Coinbase (CBDC), True USD (TUSD) and Paxos Standard (PAX).

Stake - To support the security and operations of a network, "staking" is done to keep funds locked in a cryptocurrency wallet and rewards can be earned.

An example of staking is when signing up for a Crypto.com debit card, users are required to stake $50 within the company's crypto CRO for a certain amount of time. There is no monthly or annual fee, but after the staking window has ended, users can have access to their initial stake to withdraw, invest elsewhere or leave their position within the CRO. Staking can be looked at as collateral in some respects but ultimately helps the ecosystem of the crypto being staked.

Tank - Slang that has been adopted from traditional financial markets to describe the strong negative financial performance of a specific asset.

Example: Litecoin is tanking right now, should I sell or wait?

Whale - Investors and corporations who hold a vast amount of cryptocurrency (millions or billions worth). Their portfolio has a lot of influence within the market when they buy or sell a position that they can potentially manipulate prices to dramatically increase or decrease the overall price of the crypto.

White Paper - A document created by the developers of a coin to introduce a comprehensive guide to the overall purpose and goals of a project when a new coin is introduced to the market. The document is also introduced before an ICO to pique the curiosity of investors in hopes that many would invest in the launch.

4

How Much Crypto Does It Take to Power a Lightbulb?

*"Energy consumption matters both to our environment
and our economy."*

- John Baldacci

A s cryptocurrencies become more well known, a major attack on the sector is the assumption that all cryptocurrencies are destroying the planet by the vast consumption of electricity used to power the crypto ecosystem. To dig deep into this topic, Sid John Leopold and Niclas Englesson from the College of Stockholm and Stanford, published a research paper on the carbon footprint of money. The study covered the environmental effects on Bitcoin (BTC), Ethereum (ETH), Ripple (XRP) and the Visa network, which proved XRP's superiority as the leading cryptocurrency that is eco-friendly. Contrastingly, Bitcoin poses the biggest threat by having the worst negative environmental effects. The paper compared the energy usage in layman's terms for readers to truly grasp the vast scale of energy consumption in a way readers could imagine and the below bar chart showcases the shocking results.

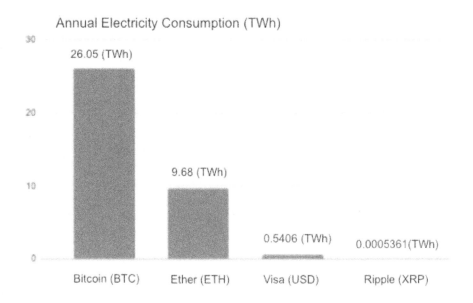

Annual Electricity Consumption (TWh)

To put into perspective how vast 1 TeraWatt Hour (TWh) truly is, the paper stated that the whole country of Scotland has a population of roughly 5 million citizens that requires 25 TWh of electrical energy per year. The paper highlighted that due to Bitcoin and Ethereum's blockchain where all coins have yet to be mined, the energy needed to power the mining activities is the pivotal factor driving the high usage of electricity within both digital currencies. However, in cases where cryptos do not require mining such as XRP and XLM, the energy consumption is far less of a threat, which makes these two cryptos eco-friendly.

Leopold and Englesson stated that if Bitcoin was a country, "it would be ranked 67th in the world by energy consumption" since mining one Bitcoin (900 are mined per day) equals the same amount of energy it takes to power 3.67 US homes per day. Below is also a similar table used within the paper to showcase the difference within the number of lightbulbs, dishwashers and driven car miles that could be powered by the energy use of 220M transactions.

	Lightbulb	Dishwashers	Car Mileage
Bitcoin	149 M	70 M	115 M
Ethereum	69 M	32 M	52 M
Visa	8,177	3,826	6 M
XRP	14	6	11,018

The staggering comparisons provided in the paper really put into perspective how the leading cryptos compare on an energy consumption level and how there is a vast environmental imprint between Bitcoin, Ethereum, XRP and Visa. To shed a contrarian perspective about Bitcoins' high energy consumption, the reputable crypto YouTube channel Altcoin Daily stated that the Christmas light industry and the video game industry are in fact more of a carbon footprint threat to the environment than Bitcoin. The YouTuber asked, "is the value that we get from this worth it in terms of energy consumption? Absolutely in my opinion." The video game industry will always thrive and Christmas wouldn't be Christmas if we didn't have any Christmas lights. So, in terms of cryptocurrencies, the same concept of value applies…depending on a person's perspective. Choosing the lesser of all evils is ultimately the best way forward to tackling a lower carbon footprint, but depending on the person or organisation, there will be mixed views regarding this topic since Bitcoin is valuable. To conclude Leopold and Englesson's paper, they explained:

> *"Money should increase efficiency no matter what trust model the currency uses. It needs to be efficient in order to have a chance of being widely adopted and functional for us all and the planet Earth. Our aim is not to embrace or discredit any model of trust on the basis of its trust component alone. We would rather state that if there is trust (regardless of model enabling it), the main value driver behind this trusted asset is going to be its utility and scalability along with the costs associated with further utilization and scaling of this asset. In this frame of reference, Ripple's XRP is way ahead of its current competition."*

To give insight into what the future holds in regard to sustainable finance, the World Economic Forum holds an annual summit called the Davos Agenda, which brings together the world's leading figures in finance and governments to target solutions for making the economy more equitable, sustainable and inclusive. Ripple CEO Brad Garlinghouse, Donald Trump, European Central Bank President Christine Lagarde and Michael Bloomberg, who co-founded the financial information and media company Bloomberg LP, were amongst the key speakers at the 2020 summit. Bloomberg was vocal about green technologies and how sustainable finance can unlock trillions that are tied up within Nostro Vostro accounts, which are pre-funded accounts institutions use specifically for international payments.

Interestingly enough, this positions XRP on a pedestal against BTC and ETH since Ripple's FinTech was specifically designed to eliminate the need for Nostro Vostro accounts in a timely and cost-effective manner, while also being eco-friendly. If XRP is used as the dominant bridge currency on a global scale, this allows the trillions locked up in Nostro Vostro accounts to become available for public funding and investments. That right there should be a no-brainer for institutions to gravitate towards Ripple's FinTech since both Bitcoin and Ether take longer to transfer value, is costly and worst of all, is harmful to the environment. This does not discredit Bitcoin or Ether's utility and longevity, but on an environmental stance, XRP is far superior by being the most environmentally friendly cryptocurrency on the market.

While discussions of a controversial "global reset" have now hit the main-stream to reset the global economy after the COVID-19 pandemic, the 2021 Davos Agenda highlighted 'Resetting Digital Currencies' as a key theme to assure that sustainable digital finances were still a main priority as part of tackling a greener future. The Bank of England's Governor Andrew Bailey was amongst the key figures to discuss their opinions on the rise of digital currencies but had a negative outlook on Bitcoin. He claimed that Bitcoin is not the future for digital payments and interestingly enough, has been quite vocal that there is a distinct problem with how expensive cross-border payments are. Although Bitcoin is a great store of value and a hedge against inflation, those in power can use the narrative of Bitcoin not being eco-friendly as a way to diminish the crypto and excuse the longevity of Bitcoin, rather than admitting that Bitcoin poses a threat due to its decentralisation. When joining the European Central Bank, Christine Lagarde took a stance on making climate change a priority and has also been vocal about her hatred towards Bitcoin, while being an advocate for Central Bank Digital Currencies (CBDC) and XRP. Regardless of any hidden agendas to pull the rug from Bitcoin, Christine Lagarde has publicly stated that they are looking into cryptocurrencies that are using distributed ledger technology that are "far from Bitcoin."

By trying to connect the dots even more, Brad Garlinghouse and Denelle Dixon, the CEO and Executive Director of the Stellar Development Foundation, are also on the World Economic Forum's Global Future Council on Cryptocurrencies. Other powerhouse members include Jose Fernandez (VP, Global Business Development, PayPal), Cuy Sheffield (Head of Crypto, Visa), Oli Harris (Vice-President, Digital Assets, Goldman Sachs), Paul Maley (MD Deutsche Bank), Christine Moy (Global Head of Liink, JPMorgan Chase & Co) and 23 other key figures within the crypto space. As part of a leading internationally recognised organisation that is committed to shaping the future of sustainable finance, it creates a very strong case for both XRP and XLM to increase its global adoption.

As we transition into the new quantum financial system, the challenge of battling carbon emissions continues to grow as the negative effects of climate change worsen. With the International Monetary Fund (IMF), European Central Bank (ECB), World Economic Forum (WEF) and the Biden administration for instance, being vocal on combating climate change, technological advancements moving into the new decade has been a key focus to a more inclusive and greener future. With the U.S. signing back into the Paris agreement in 2021 due to the Biden administration in office, this international treaty binds the 197 countries that have signed the agreement in an aim to tackle the hurdles of climate change. Since the Biden administration is more environmentally conscious than the Republican Party, choosing to use an eco-friendly cryptocurrency such as XRP and XLM over Bitcoin as a new world reserve currency or as a bridged currency, positions both cryptos as the front running digital currencies to lead a new monetary landscape as we transition through the fourth industrial revolution.

5

Crypto Exchanges

*"What we want is fully anonymous, ultra-low transaction cost
and transferable units of exchange. If we get that going...
the banks will become the obsolete dinosaurs they deserve to become."*

– Adam Back

F uelled with excitement to take the leap of faith and invest, the next concern is where to get your hands on crypto. Similar to traditional stock exchanges such as the New York Stock Exchange (NYSE), London Stock Exchange (LSE) or the Shanghai Stock Exchange (SSE) for instance, the various online crypto focused exchanges allow investors to buy, hold and sell but also to store, send, convert and receive cryptocurrency. Instead of anxiously waiting for the NYSE bell to ring at 9:30 AM (EST) to begin a day of trading and to close off trades by 4:00 PM (EST), crypto investors have the freedom to trade on exchanges 24/7 including on weekends, which is a favourable bonus the crypto sector has over the stock market.

The best way to regard exchanges is to think of it as a matchmaking bridge between a buyer and a seller. When someone wants to sell their position within a crypto and a buyer wants to sink their teeth into the same crypto, these exchanges automatically match the two investors together to complete a transaction. Depending on the technicality an investor requires for an exchange, there are a handful of various exchanges to choose from. This chapter will focus on the popular exchanges that beginners tend to lean towards.

Coinbase

Coinbase's mission statement is to "be the most trusted and easiest to use" centralised exchange in the sector. A remarkable achievement the exchange has highlighted on its website is that more than 35 million people in over 100 countries trust Coinbase to buy, sell, store, send and earn cryptocurrency. Nonetheless, Coinbase has lived up to its expectations as the most recognisable exchange on an international basis since it is geared towards beginner investors who want to get their hands on the most common cryptocurrencies. Those who are gravitated towards this exchange are typically investors who don't want the process to be too technical since the app and online site is easy to navigate. Users can link their bank card and can automate payments on a daily, weekly or monthly basis which is a great option for those who want to invest a certain amount every month to reduce risk against trying to time the market.

Coinbase contains all the favorable coins that beginners are drawn to - Bitcoin, Ethereum, Stellar Lumen, Quant, Algorand, Shiba Inu, Litecoin, Chainlink and a few other coins are amongst the short list of coins available. XRP used to be listed on the exchange, but due to the current lawsuit with the SEC, the exchange suspended trading in January 2021 until regulations become clear.

In addition to the exchange's main functionalities, the main website has a directory of resources for beginners to learn basic information of the coins listed on the exchange and can shed light into some troubling questions beginners may have. An intriguing feature the site offers is the ability to watch short videos to learn about numerous cryptocurrencies to earn free crypto as a reward for watching said videos. You can use the link below to watch a few quick videos (not more than 5 minutes) to learn about Stellar Lumen and receive $10 for free.

https://bit.ly/2KGfivm

The newest feature Coinbase introduced is a physical crypto debit card. Users can load the card with any cryptocurrency to spend, with the ability to withdraw fiat from ATMs. In the span of a year after the inception of the debit card in April 2019, Coinbase praised on Twitter that collectively over a million dollars' worth of purchases have been made worldwide. The only downfall of the card are the various fees linked, which is highly recommended to look into before applying for the debit card.

Whilst writing this book during 2020, the initial mission statement Coinbase set out to "be the most trusted and easiest to use," had a few controversial slips for the public to question the exchanges transparency. The Black

Lives Matter (BLM) movement propelled a few employees from Coinbase to publicly share their experience of discrimination as people of colour working at Coinbase. A piece written by the New York Times titled, "Tokenized: Inside Black Workers' Struggles at the King of Crypto Start-Ups," exposed the truth behind closed doors for those who are curious to read further.

To add to the dodginess on a front-end functionality, the exchange also sneakily took away the feature for investors to set price alerts and is notorious for having technical issues when the price of Bitcoin spikes to hit an all-time high due to the large volume of users on Coinbase. You'd think after a few years that they would use a plethora of the fees pumped into the exchange to solve a simple flow of traffic issue, but no – it's become a vicious cycle.

Coinbase has red flags on an ethical level, but still continues to be the most popular exchange for beginners to use due to its global popularity and ease of use. At least they got one half of their mission statement correct – to be the "easiest to use" exchange. If you do, however, want to sign up to Coinbase for free due to its ease of use, you can use the promo link below to get $10 when you apply.

https://bit.ly/2M6CAL7

Binance

Binance is the world's biggest centralised exchange that has more advanced features than Coinbase and has a vast menu of over 150 plus cryptos to choose from with lower trading fees. Those who are no stranger to trading stocks or crypto would ease into Binance's platform right away, however, beginners may find that a bit more effort is needed to understand the technical features from a first glance. Not to be discouraged, the exchange offers a free 'Binance Academy' section on the main website that offers a helpful guide and is also a hub for learning about the sector.

The Binance Academy also offers a more in-depth A-Z glossary of the top 265 technical terms within the sector for those that want to dive a bit more down the rabbit hole. In addition to learning the basic features on the site, the academy also offers tutorials for more risky and advanced investors with instructions on how to leverage and use Binance Loans to earn interest on crypto and tutorials on how to trade Futures. Those who want to test their technical crypto knowledge can also partake in quizzes available through the academy that cater to beginners, intermediates or advanced investors.

For the whales who have a bit more cheddar to slap on the table, Binance offers no trading fees through an "over-the-counter" (OTC) portal for those who want to invest more than USD 10,000 in a trade. Depositing money is completely free, however, for every trade that is not OTC, Binance takes a 0.1% cut which is a reasonable fee for the exchange's services. A huge selling point of Binance is that the exchange offers financial services where users can take out crypto loans and even earn interest for 'lending' crypto to margin traders to earn up to 15% as a reward. This is a great way to make a passive income for those who have a long-term plan of holding a certain crypto.

To add to the plethora of functionalities, the exchange recently announced its partnership with Stripe and Simplex to release a crypto debit card, similar to the Coinbase offering that is valid wherever Visa and Mastercard is accepted. There will be no monthly fees, but an upsetting factor of the card are the high fees at 3.5% per transaction or 10 USD, depending on the higher option. The fees alone would dig a hole in your pocket which is a turnoff to have as an everyday spending account. However, using the card for larger one-off purchases would be more ideal out of convenience for those who are interested.

With all the features mentioned above along with the exchange offering occasional competitions with rewards, makes Binance one of the dominant exchanges with over 15 million users worldwide with approximately USD 2 billion worth of trades a day. Although there are a lot of positives about

Binance, there has been some negative news targeting the exchange within the UK mid 2021. The online crypto community went into a frenzy when news circulated that Binance is now banned within the UK, however, the truth of the matter is that the mainstream media spread false claims without properly digging into the matter. Long story short, investors are still able to trade cryptos within the UK on the exchange but leverage trading futures, margin and derivatives for instance is not permitted. Lastly, due to Ripple's lawsuit, Binance US has delisted XRP, but Binance for the rest of the world still has XRP live for trading.

You can use the link below to sign up for a free Binance account, which we both make a 10% kickback off the fees for each trade.

https://bit.ly/3cMeVLf

Crypto.com

Crypto.com is the newest centralised exchange to enter the sector and their mission is to catapult the world's ease of transition into the cryptocurrency spectrum. At first, I was skeptical since the exchange seemed too good to be true, but after a lot of research and even emailing Visas' partnership program, I became a fan and less of a skeptic.

The allure of the exchange is heavily focused on trading, lending programs and the ability to earn flexible savings. However, the real kicker is the notorious Visa-based debit card that offers lower fees than other exchanges. The card offers cash back rewards (1%-5%) and membership perks depending on the chosen card. Perks include free Spotify and Netflix accounts for cheaper cards, while the more exclusive rewards include an Amazon Prime membership, LoungeKey airport lounge services, private jet access, Expedia and Airbnb discounts. The only negative I have experienced so far is that it took me 3 months to receive my Visa debit card, so if you're debating on applying, be patient.

A downfall for some users is that in order to reap the rewards offered, users have to 'stake' the exchanges own tokens (CRO and/or MCO) but realistically this just keeps the ecosystem afloat. Standard fees are a rate of a 0.1% maker fee and 0.16% taker fee, but additional discounted rates are given to larger trade volumes. Less than 20 cryptos are currently available for trading and it is also one of the exchanges to delist XRP during the lawsuit. When it comes to security, all users' cryptocurrencies are stored on an offline wallet which relies on the security features from a popular hardware wallet company called Ledger. Lastly, another intriguing allure is that the exchange secured a $360 million insurance policy to protect users against security breaches.

To sign up for a free Crypto.com account, you can use the below link to get $30 as part of their promotion:

https://bit.ly/2XaHkoC

Decentralised Exchanges (DEX)

The main functions of an exchange are to match orders, deposit capital and to have an order book. In order for a decentralised exchange to operate, these three points need to also be decentralised to cut the middleman of an intermediary, such as Coinbase or Binance for instance, out of the picture for a digital asset exchange. This creates a platform for peer-to-peer transactions that is run by users. Centralised exchanges take a trading fee due to the ease of use, whereas decentralised exchanges allow traders to swap coins directly between each other. This eliminates the need for a trading fee as it is similar to the transfer process of sending money from our bank account to a friend who also has a local bank account.

Due to anti-laundering regulations and the know-your-customer formality of centralised exchanges, customers need to confirm their identification and place of residence before an account can be approved, whereas this is not a requirement through decentralised exchanges. DEXes are a great option for those who live in countries that have strong regulations that pertain to cryptocurrency as it offers a way for investors to still be a part of the market. This is not to be taken in a doggy stance, but rather if people don't have the required passport or driver's license for approval for instance, they could be rejected from a centralised exchange.

An issue when it comes to centralised exchanges is that the companies behind the exchanges could be subjected to bankruptcy, hacks or shut down due to force majeure, which creates a risk for the crypto held on those exchanges. There have been incidents in the past where less popular centralised exchanges have been hacked or had to shut down. This left users at a loss with their crypto that was held on the exchanges. Decentralised exchanges mitigate these risks since any blockchain that is built on a decentralised exchange cannot be shut down due to the coding and lack of intermediary authority. Unless the whole chain is shut down which is challenging to do, that's the only way a DEX can be taken down.

A few flaws when it comes to decentralised exchanges is that trading large amounts can be difficult since there usually is a lower amount of liquidity on decentralised exchanges, which can cause the order process to be slower than centralised exchanges. Patience and further due diligence are needed when using decentralised exchanges as each DEX varies depending on which crypto you want to trade, unlike a centralised exchange like Binance that has everything in one place. If you prefer staying under the raider and taking your crypto in your own hands, then decentralised exchanges is the perfect fit. However, if you prefer a more seamless way to ease into the market, then a centralised exchange like Binance would be suitable to fight off the beginner nerves that many tend to have.

Although there is a trading fee involved, a centralised exchange usually gives beginners more confidence since they can feel more connected to a company rather than a network run by strangers. Decentralised exchanges offer more control over your crypto, however, a downfall for beginners who have yet to enter the market may find DEXes challenging to use as the majority are not user-friendly right off the bat. In addition, DEXes are mostly targeted to those who already have crypto and want to trade their position. Nonetheless, a beginner friendly DEX is stellarx.com that allows users to link their bank or credit card to purchase crypto, which also gives the option to trade BTC, ETH, XLM and XRP peer-to-peer. Contrastingly, the majority of other decentralised exchanges is based on Ethereum's blockchain that caters to various DApps, which means cryptos such as XRP, XLM, BTC, ADA for instance will be harder to trade. A list of a variety of decentralised exchanges can be found below as a reference of the most popular choices.

- Sologenic.org
- Interstellar.exchange
- Xrptoolkit.com
- Atomex.me
- Bisq.network
- Jelly.market
- Liquality.io
- Uniswap.org
- Gatehub.net
- Idex.io
- 0x.org
- Airswap.io
- Bancor.network
- Kyber.network
- Idex.market
- Paradex.io
- Radarrelay.com

Depending on the kind of investor you are, the requirements you seek for an exchange and your geographical region plays a big part when choosing exchanges. Using the above information is a good starting point to gear you towards doing your own due diligence to see which exchange you resonate with.

Coinbase may be easier to sign up for those living in Australia, the UK and Europe but can be harder for those in Canada, which pushes Canadians towards other exchanges such as Bitbuy or Kucoin. Americans may have trouble signing up to Binance, so it forces a lot of Americans to use Coinbase, Uphold, Crypto.com, Bitmex or Kraken. Gemini is also another exchange, which was created by the infamous Facebook Winklevoss twins and is highly popular within the US and South America with lower fees, but is limited to only a few international countries. CoinSwitch is the top exchange within India whereas Paxful is the largest peer-to-peer Bitcoin marketplace in the world, but only commonly used within Africa. Lastly, if you're based in Asia, then Remitano or Bitfinex would be a popular choice.

If you're from the US, UK or Europe and interested in investing in XRP where a lot of exchanges have suspended or delisted XRP during the duration of the SEC lawsuit, then Uphold is the preferred exchange. The CEO of Uphold has also been very vocal online in support of Ripple during the lawsuit as he is very confident that XRP is not a security as the SEC claims, so Uphold has become the new trusted go-to exchange for XRP fans. Once regulatory clarity is given for XRP, exchanges should start re-listing the crypto back on the exchanges it was taken down from such as Coinbase and Crypto.com.

For a promo link to sign up to Uphold, you can use the link below:

https://bit.ly/3yw1YwD

Exchange Tips:

- For an extra layer of protection, it is recommended to not use SMS authentication as hackers can 'SIM Swap' to try and intercept the authentication process if they have access to your phone number. A

71

safer alternative is to download the Authy, Duo Security or Google Authenticator app directly on your mobile. The app links to your exchanges to confirm your identity upon sign in rather than using an SMS for confirmation. It may sound complicated, but it is really easy and tutorials can be found on YouTube for ease of mind.

- Set up price alerts on your exchange's app for your investments so you can always track price fluctuations and you can even go the extra mile to set a 'stop loss' on trades. This is an order placed before placing a purchase or sale once the coin reaches a certain price.

- There is no rule that you have to stick to one exchange. Some users stick to one while others use more than one – it is completely dependent on the investor themselves. Prices of cryptos vary on every exchange as well, so take advantage of having multiple accounts to spread your wealth and go the extra mile to try and snatch the best deal. For example, you can buy crypto on Binance due to the cheaper fees, but then send it to your Crypto.com account to keep it on the exchanges offline wallet if you don't have a hardware wallet.

- Stay away from using Robinhood as an exchange. Investors using the app do not technically own their own position as it's more like an IOU and the app can revoke your trades at any moment. Robinhood also received backlash in early 2021 after the Wall Street Bets fiasco where the app halted trading of certain stocks and cryptos that were favourable for retail investors to gain profit. Robinhood has been notorious in the past for manipulating the market to protect banks and hedge funds, which drove retail investors into an outrage to write a sea of negative reviews online. As a result, the company went on a mass deleting spree and deleted over 100,000 bad reviews in early 2021. Red flag galore.

- The best solution to keep any crypto safe regardless of if it was purchased on a centralised exchange, is to purchase a hardware wallet where you can safely store your crypto to keep it offline. This will be discussed in more detail within the next chapter.

6

Crypto Wallets

"Keep your friends close,
your enemies closer
and your wallets even closer."

- Joette Rockow

W hen getting into cryptocurrency, it is beneficial to know the various ways of managing your crypto by using a 'hot' or 'cold' wallet. Just how we have physical wallets where we store our cards, fiat money or photos of your children, a cryptocurrency wallet is the same concept where you can safely store your crypto, whilst also being able to send and receive crypto to others. The best way to view hot and cold wallets is to compare an everyday banking account to a savings account. Hot wallets would be the equivalent to your everyday banking account as you wouldn't leave all your money in the account but use the money casually. Cold wallets would be similar to a savings account since you have a large chunk of your crypto stored that you don't regularly touch for safe keeping.

A hot wallet is in reference to any *online* wallet where you can store your cryptocurrency. This can include wallets directly on the various exchanges or software applications such as exodus.io that uses the internet to store crypto online. While crypto can be left in a personal digital wallet on centralised exchanges, this still gives the exchange control over your digital assets, which can also be targeted by hackers.

The most effective wallet that has proven to be safest is a "cold hardware wallet" since it is an offline device. These physical devices resemble a USB stick, but contain a screen and buttons for navigation to use passwords (private keys) to keep your crypto safe on a device that is not connected to the internet, which means it is not susceptible to hacks. It is important to note that although buying and selling on exchanges is credible, transferring crypto to a device that is not linked to an internet connection adds a superior layer of protection from potential hackers after you have made trades. The only way someone can access your crypto on a cold hardware wallet is if you give them access to your private keys and even if a wallet is lost or stolen, a new one can be purchased to link the same private keys. This is why keeping passwords offline is pivotal to effectively shield yourself from becoming a hacking target. Physically write your private keys down, laminate it, put it in a box, find a private hiding spot to dig a hole to dump the box and cover it back with dirt. This is an extreme example but people will go through leaps and bounds to keep their passwords safe. Do whatever you need to do to make copies and safely store those codes, otherwise, if you can't remember your passwords then you unfortunately don't have access to your cryptocurrency. Whoever controls the private keys, controls the crypto attached to those passwords. Now that you're familiar with what a hot and a cold wallet is, the next step is to find out the two dominant cold wallets and see which one you prefer.

Ledger Nano S is the most affordable yet effective wallet on the market for £52.00 (VAT included) with access to 1100 different cryptocurrencies. It is also simple to navigate which makes this wallet the best-selling option for beginners to familiarise themselves with. TREZOR One (€70.51 VAT included) used to be the dominant wallet in the sector until the Ledger Nano S came and stole the title. For a few pounds more, the TREZOR One screen is bigger, however, the wallet currently carries 100 coins less than the Ledger Nano S.

There are more similarities to the two wallets than differences, however, the major difference between the two is that the Ledger Nano S uses proprietary software while TREZOR uses a web interface. There are more advanced models from both manufacturers depending on the accessible needs you want from a wallet as well – i.e., managing more than 5 crypto assets on one device, bigger touch screens or even the ability to use Bluetooth for instance. If these advancements interest you then you can look into the Ledger Nano X (£109.00) or the TREZOR T (€178.80).

As tempting as it may be to try and shop around online, it is imperative to only purchase these cold wallets directly from the main manufacturers' websites. You put yourself at risk for hackers to sabotage the device if you use a pre-owned device or allow a third-party company or website to handle these devices before it reaches you. It is also crucial to only download the recommended software for wallets directly from the manufacturers' main website and not off other sites or app stores to reduce security breaches.

When writing this book, Ledger unfortunately experienced a shocking data breach where hackers gained access to customer's contact details. Although this seems terrifying at first, it's a great learning curve of how to take precaution to always be a step ahead of hackers. I am going to repeat myself by saying this, but just to reiterate, people can only access the crypto attached to your hardware wallet if you give someone your private keys. The actual device will always remain safe since it is an offline device, but hackers can create fake email accounts and phone numbers posing as wallet companies to mislead users to willingly handover their private keys. Regardless of what wallet company you buy from, a company will NEVER ask you to send your private keys, crypto payments or send a link to fill out a form to change your account details. Hackers feed off of fear so if an email appears fishy, the best thing to do is to report it - don't click any links and do not reply.

The emails I have received from Ledger, for instance, have always been from a no-reply address (noreply@ledger.com) or a customer service support email (support@ledger.zendesk.com), so always double check the addresses for clarity if the body of the email seems out of the ordinary. This is where common sense comes into the picture because if Ledger is sending an email from a Gmail account, that's automatically a red flag. In addition, wallet companies do not use SMS as a customer service option, so that is another red flag to keep in mind. In situations like these data breaches, a helpful site to double check if your email address has been compromised or if there are any data breaches is haveibeenpwned.com. If you have unfortunately been a victim, immediately change your email address on all crypto accounts. In addition, always make sure you have 2-factor authentication set up with a third party authenticator (Google or Authy for instance) in combination with a strong password by having at least 16 characters that includes uppercase, lowercase, numbers and special characters.

To prevent any data breaches, it is imperative when signing up for any crypto related sites or when purchasing a wallet, to never enter a telephone number and to only use an email that was created for crypto related matters. By having no trace of your phone number attached to any crypto related account or within any emails, lessens the risk of hackers to "SIM Swap."

If you hold a lot of crypto, the last way to keep it safe is by spreading your wealth across multiple wallets and to keep all devices and written passwords separate. Some people who hold a vast amount go the extra mile to keep wallets in separate countries, different security boxes and in scattered locations within their residential area. Depending on how much crypto you have, taking these extra steps can go a long way to not put a target on yourself.

The whole wallet process may seem technical or nerve wracking at first, but there are a handful of helpful videos on YouTube with a visual step-by-step guide on how to set up the various devices. The process becomes as easy as saving files on a USB stick once you get the hang of it, but if you have any burning questions stemming from the initial confusion wallets may bring, the manufacturers' main site does a good job of putting everything into perspective. Although I was one of the customers whose data was breached, Ledger still remains my preferred offline wallet as the device itself is safer than leaving crypto on an exchange, it's easy to navigate and I've followed the above precautions to stay safe.

For those that love a bargain, the main Ledger website usually runs promotions where you can occasionally receive 20% off, especially around holidays as a promotion. Although the price tag attached to these wallets may seem like a steep purchase, the long-term benefits outweigh the one-time price tag. If you want to test your luck, crypto YouTuber Crypto Zombie has a partnership with Ledger where every Monday he gives a free Ledger Nano S to someone who has commented on his daily videos throughout the previous week. You can comment as many times as possible and anxiously hope to be a lucky winner. If that doesn't interest you then you can simply buy one yourself or just fully pass on the wallet and keep your money on an exchange hoping no one hacks it. There is no golden rule that you have to use cold wallets as it is simply a safe precaution you can take to make sure your crypto is secured offline. If you have more crypto on an exchange than you're willing to lose, then it is highly recommended to use one, but ultimately it is down to the investor to make this decision for themselves. As my mother always says – "it's better to be safe, than sorry."

Promo Links for Wallets

Ledger Nano S Starter Pack - includes hardware wallet, free crypto guide and $25 voucher to purchase crypto: bit.ly/3fgHS1B

TREZOR One: bit.ly/3w3Xgoz

TREZOR Model T: bit.ly/3y84pq3

7

Where to Get Information?

"The reason people succeed is that they have knowledge other people don't."

- Tony Robbins

With the crypto market open 24/7, comes a strong online community that circulates a consistent flow of information on a daily basis. Although the sector can be overwhelming for beginners, knowing where to get the right information is key. This chapter will provide a guide on where you can easily retain information to do your own due diligence and to keep up to date with the sector.

Main Source for Crypto News

To get to the very core of insightful articles, technical analysis and speculative opinions, the below sources are the leading sites to stay up to date with crypto specific news. The remaining 40 sites that are ranked by users of Detailed can be found on at detailed.com/cryptocurrency-blogs.

Top 5:

1. Cointelegraph.com
2. Coindesk.com
3. U.today
4. News.bitcoin.com
5. Newsbtc.com

Real Vision

Real Vision was created by my favourite Global Macro Investor Raoul Pal – just how people look up to rock stars, Pal is the John Lennon of the crypto space. By having more than 30 years of experience within the financial markets, in which he was a former Goldman Sachs Exec, Pal has become a key figure within the crypto space due to his relaxed, concise and in-depth approach to breaking down the fundamentals of the global economics, business and financial markets in a comprehensible manner. By having a team of the "world's top macro-researchers," Real Vision provides investors with in-depth interviews, research, newsletters, documentaries, analysis and trade ideas in which the same exclusive level of macro analysis is provided to leading banks and hedge funds.

The below recommended videos are available after signing up for a free account via realvision.com.

Highlighted Videos:

- How Risk Management for Crypto Differs From Traditional Markets

- Abra: The Future of Crypto Banking

- Cardano: Smart Contract War Heats Up

- Portfolio and Construction: Beyond Bitcoin and Ethereum

- Aave: The Evolution of a DeFi Lending Protocol

- BlockFi: Bridging the Gap Between Traditional and Crypto

- Oasis Network: Refining Decentralized & Private Blockchain Infrastructure

- Crypto is Like A Growth Stock Dream

- Dan Tapiero: Three Key Crypto Investment Categories

- Yield Curve Control, Non-Fungible Tokens (NFTs) & Wobbling Equity Market w/Raoul

Podcasts

Podcasts are a great source of falling down the rabbit hole of research and staying up to date on the market. Many feature interviews from experts within the field, which is always interesting to hear an insightful perspective straight from the horses' mouth. Listen while you're travelling, cooking, taking a shower or even trying to head to dream land, podcasts are a great way to retain information while on the go or relaxing in the comfort of your own home. Below are the top choices that are easy for beginners to follow.

The Pomp Podcast by Anthony Pompliano (Apple and YouTube)

Anthony Pompliano is a popular name within the crypto community and is known for appearing on CNBC going head-to-head with Kevin O'Leary on why Bitcoin is a valuable asset. His 400 plus episodes contain interviewers with billionaires Mark Cuban and Chamath Palihapitiya, who are fervent investors in Bitcoin, along with a wide selection of topics that range from business, finance and Bitcoin. He also hosts a 20-minute YouTube segment everyday with his wife called, "Lunch Money" to discuss economics and business where his goal is to "help you get smarter every day." The only negative thing I'd say about Pomp is the fact that he is a hardcore Bitcoin maximalist and rarely speaks of other cryptos. Even if people may bring up negative arguments for Bitcoin, he will always divert the attention away to never have a contrarian view.

Highlighted Episodes:

- Ep. 444: Hedge Fund Millionaire Invests All His Money in Bitcoin | Raoul Pal

- Ep. 439: Brad Garlinghouse (Ripple CEO) on Crypto Regulation

- Ep. 317: Soona Amhaz On The Future of Crypto Outside The US

- Ep. 256: Billionaire Chamath Palihapitiya on How To Invest in This Crisis

- Ep. 301: Travis Kling on the Future of Bitcoin

- Ep. 294: Cullen Roche Explains The Ultimate Breakdown Of The Federal Reserve

- Ep. 285: Dan Held on Bitcoin and the Halving

- Ep. 263: Robert Kiyosaki on How The World's Wealthiest Invest Their Money

Unchained and Unconfirmed by Laura Shin (Apple, Google and YouTube)

Laura is an iconic figure within a male dominated industry. She gained a lot of respect by being the Editor of Forbes Crypto and whilst being the go-to expert at Forbes, she juggled her Unchained podcast on the side as a labour of love. With the rise in success from the podcast, she left her position at Forbes to focus on the podcast full time and now has another podcast called Unconfirmed under her belt. Unchained is specifically geared towards discussing new ideas within the sector, while Unconfirmed features interviews with experts within the field.

Unchained Highlighted Episodes:

- Ep. 177: Christopher Giancarlo: Why the US Needs to Have a Digital Dollar

- Ep. 176: Rep. Warren Davidson: 'I Think Bitcoin Is a Great Store of Value'

- Ep. 172: The Third Bitcoin Halving Just Happened: What Now?

- Ep. 162: Why Africa Is Poised to Be the Next Hub for Crypto Development

- Ep. 97: How Crypto and Blockchain Technology Could Change Financial Services

Unconfirmed Highlighted Episodes:

- Ep. 124: A Bitcoin Price of $115,000 Next Year?

- Ep. 84: The IRS Is Cracking Down on Crypto Taxes: What You Need to Know

- Ep. 163: Why Asia Is So Important to Crypto

- Ep. 162: Why the GameStop Insanity Is So Similar to Crypto

Bitcoin Audible by Guy Swann (Apple & Spotify)

This series aims to make "the knowledge of the world's most secure, independent money accessible to everyone."

Highlighted Episodes:

- Ep. 390: Bitcoin is Common Sense [Parker Lewis]

- Ep. 385: Bitcoin & the Technological Evolution of the Financial System [BitcoinTINA]

- Ep. 36: How the Dollar Destroys Society with Bottom Shelf Bitcoin

- Ep. 34: The Great Wealth Transfer with Pete Rizzo

- Ep. 498: Can Governments Stop Bitcoin? [Alex Gladstein]

Crypto 101 by Bryce Paul & Pizza Mind (Apple)

Their tagline says it all - 'the average consumers' guide to cryptocurrency.'

Highlighted Episodes:

- Ep. 331: Dollar Cost Averaging w/ Cory Klipstein from Swan Bitcoin

- Ep. 327: What are "derivatives" (options & futures) & Why They Matter, w/ Phemex CEO

- Ep. 272: Bitcoin Matters for Your Freedom and Future

- Ep. 257: No BS with "Bitcoin Pizza" Author Samantha Radocchia

The Breakdown by Nathaniel Whittemore (Apple, Spotify & Coindesk)

Co-produced by Coindesk, The Breakdown provides a daily dose of three crypto topics with each episode lasting 15 minutes or less.

Highlighted Episodes:

- No, the Digital Dollar Won't Kill Bitcoin

- Are NFTs Just This Cycle's ICOs

- How Nigeria and India Are Dealing With Crypto Bans

- Is Janet Yellen Bitcoin's Biggest Enemy or Greatest Asset?

- Goldman Sachs Can No Longer Dismiss Bitcoin

- Why I Changed My Mind on Bitcoin

YouTube

Aside from the funny videos of animals and obnoxious videos you get sucked into at 2 AM, YouTube is a useful platform to learn about various topics. Most YouTubers post videos every week, but because the crypto sector is open 24/7, the majority of crypto influencers put out a video every single day or every other day. The alluring pull of these influencers is that they make learning about the sector visually appealing by having a creative and entertaining flair to absorb information. Although it needs to be noted that they are NOT financial advisors - they are simply investors who express their opinions, do technical analysis, share news and articles based on their own due diligence. As controversial as YouTubers can be due to a preconceived notion that they lack credibility, these crypto channels are a prime example of how the platform is an exceptional way of teaching yourself information without spending an arm and a leg for a course.

As amazing as YouTube is though, a recent downfall of the platform is that the site is cracking down on "shadow-banning" and even banning content that pushes individuals to think outside the box. Instead of the site deleting videos off the platform, shadow-banning is the execution of the algorithm blocking certain keywords within the crypto sector from searches or popping up on the side as a recommendation of interest. As a result, there have been numerous times where users record themselves subscribing to crypto channels and instantly go back to the channel, to find that the site automatically unsubscribes users from crypto channels. Due to the obvious meddling in free speech on the platform, it is recommended to actually subscribe and sign up to the alerts of the influencers you are drawn to.

In a sector that is quickly changing, it is interesting to hear other investors' perspectives about the sector to pique your interest to doing further due diligence. I've seen a comment on a respected crypto YouTuber's video of this woman complaining because she bought a crypto that an influencer talked about and when the price dropped after she bought it, she panicked and sold her position. She then played the blame game to try and warn people of this 'scammer' in the comment section, but funnily enough, received a backlash of harsh responses since we can't blame anyone but ourselves for the investment decisions we make. Little did she know that if she would have not panicked, sold and held onto the crypto longer, she would have made a higher return, but she got nervous and tried to deflect her own blame. It is moments like this to remember that there is a lot of information floating around online, but it's how we receive, learn and choose to adapt the information presented that influences our actions. If influencers are shilling (promoting) coins to buy, then take it with a grain of salt to always use critical thinking and continue to do your own research before investing. This allows you to be confident with your portfolio – otherwise you are gambling with your money.

Crypto Casey

One of the few female crypto YouTubers and has the easiest videos for beginners to learn about the sector.

Highlighted Videos:

- Blockchain Explained: What is Blockchain and How does Blockchain Technology Work?

- What is Bitcoin & How Bitcoin Works (A Simple Explanation)

- Cryptocurrency Security (Things You Need to Do BEFORE Investing in Crypto)

- How to Buy Cryptocurrency for Beginners (UPDATED Ultimate Guide)

- DeFi on Ethereum Explained - Decentralized Finance (Ultimate Beginner's Guide)

- Bitcoin Wallet: Ledger Nano S & Trezor One Hardware Wallets Step-by-Step Guide

- What are NFT's in Crypto? (Non-Fungible Tokens!) - Beginner's Guide

- Binance Exchange: How to Buy Cryptocurrency for Beginners Ultimate Step-by-Step

- Buy Bitcoin in Canada: How to Buy Cryptocurrency with BitBuy Exchange in 2021

- Stock Market Crash Soon? (What About Crypto?) - Last Week Crypto

Data Dash

Nicholas Merten is the most reputable crypto YouTuber due to his relaxed and easy approach to teaching technical analysis and giving tips on trading. He has a mix of videos catered to beginners and experienced investors.

Highlighted Videos:

- How To Simplify Investing in Bitcoin

- Trading Cryptocurrencies for Beginners

- Trading Tip #9: Three Signs To Buy A Cryptocurrency

- Trading Tip #5: Three Ways To Time The Market

- Trading Tip #10: Three Signs To Sell A Cryptocurrency

- Trading Tip #11: Three Mindsets of a Successful Investor

- Trading Tip #17: The Differences of Investing in Stocks and Cryptocurrencies

- Goldman Sachs Bashes Bitcoin | Here's What You Need To Know

Bitboy Crypto

Bitboy Crypto is a great channel for beginners to ease into the sector without feeling confused. Some of his videos in the past have highlighted how to avoid scams, how to keep your crypto safe, price predictions which also incorporates news, while also having an entertaining edge over other YouTubers.

Highlighted Videos:

- Invest Like Warren Buffett (#1 Strategy for Investment)

- How To BEST Predict Crypto Prices and Recognize Trends

- SIMPLE Ways to Make Gains (BEST Crypto Trading Hack)

- How to Analyse if Crypto is BEARISH or BULLISH

- Top Banks Are Lying About Bitcoin (They Are Buying BTC)

- How to Make Money with Crypto (5 Best Ways)

- Best Crypto Trading Strategies Explained

- Biggest Lessons from 2017 Bull Market

- Raoul Pal on Ethereum: BIGGEST Opportunity in Crypto in 2021

- When to Sell Your Cryptocurrency: Complete Guide!!

- Cardano Coin 50x EXPLOSION (One Thing Separates ADA)

- Why I'm BUYING XRP (A Ripple Love Story)

- 2021 Ultimate Tax Guide (Crypto Taxes EXPLAINED by Expert)

Alessio Rastani

Alessio is a respected trader and mentor who has 10 years of experience as a trader. Although many of his videos are geared towards technical analysis, his approach to showcasing his analysis is still inviting for beginners wanting to sink their teeth into reading charts.

Highlighted Videos:

- 3 Ways to Know When to Buy Bitcoin, Crypto, Stocks and Forex

- This Trader Lost EVERYTHING in 1 Day. Here's What Happened Next

- A Storm is Coming (Warning Signs for the Markets)

- This is How You Spot a Bull Trap (and Dangerous B-Waves)

- The Secret to Beating FOMO (Fear of Missing Out)

Altcoin Daily

Brotherly duo Austin and Aaron tag team the channel to provide live streams, news updates and eye-opening interviews with reputable names within the sector.

Highlighted Videos:

- Bitcoin's Value Proposition 2020 | EASILY EXPLAINED

- "Bitcoin Has NEVER Been Stronger In 2020. I've Waited 8 Years For This."

- Why Does Bitcoin Have Value? | "The Most Disruptive Innovation In Our Lifetime!"

- J.P. Morgan's EXTRAORDINARY Moves Into Bitcoin | The Great Crypto Conspiracy

- BREAKING: Germany Just Released The Bitcoin Bulls! Germany's Stock Exchange To List Bitcoin

Crypto Lark

The Crypto Lark covers various cryptocurrency news, analysis, reviews and interviews with reputable leaders in the field.

Highlighted Videos:

- The 4 Reasons You Lose Money Investing in Bitcoin & Crypto

- Akon Interview - Africa Needs Crypto Right Now! Don't Matter the Cost!

- Wall Street Can't Stop Buying Bitcoin - Insane Demand in 2020 - You Won't Believe This

- My 5 Biggest Bitcoin & Crypto Mistakes Explained

Working Money Channel

XRP focused channel with a mix of light technical analysis and news that pertains to the crypto.

Highlighted Videos:

- Ripple XRP: If BTC Does This, Could XRP Reach +$100/XRP By The Fall Of 2022?

- Ripple XRP: BE CAREFUL What Coins You Hold - SEC Ripple Lawsuit To Set Precedent

- Ripple XRP: John Deaton Uncovers "True Motives" For The SEC's Action To Sue Ripple

- Ripple XRP: Glenn Hutchins Describes Exactly What Ripple's Strategy Is At Davos 2021

- Ripple XRP: Is This What's Going To Bring Us To +25/XRP?

Coin Bureau

A great source for beginners and vets within the market to learn about new projects, tips and tricks for navigating through the market.

Highlighted Videos:

- TOP 10 BEST Crypto Research Tools: 2021 Edition!!

- When to SELL Your Altcoins: Complete Guide!!

- Cardano: ADA Run Could Just Be BEGINNING!!

- WATCH OUT For These Crypto Scams & Shills!!

- Latest BITCOIN BANS!! Potential Price Impact??

- Tokenomics: Difference Between 100x & Getting REKT!!

- Binance: Complete Beginner's Guide + Fee DISCOUNT

- Buying Crypto SAFELY: Complete Beginner's Guide!!

- Technical Analysis: TOP TIPS To MAX GAINS!!

- Crypto Tax Tips: ESSENTIAL GUIDE To Save Sats!!

- HOW TO DYOR: My Crypto Research Methods Revealed!!

- Technical Analysis: Everything YOU NEED TO KNOW!!

- Binance US vs. Coinbase Pro: BEST US Exchange??

- Why NFTs Could SUPERCHARGE DEFI!!

- Crypto.com Exchange: What You NEED TO KNOW!!

- Yield Farming: MAXIMISING DEFI GAINS!!

- Where to Find 100x Tokens Before It's TOO LATE!!

Digital Asset News

This channel is one of the best sources to keep up to date with news in the crypto sector.

Highlighted Videos:

• BITCOIN is the OIL & GOLD of 2020 a JAW-DROPPING Article UNCOVERS

• Why Sports & Crypto Will Be Huge. Ethereum 51% Protest By Miners?

• No Ban In India For Bitcoin And Cryptocurrency. Ethereum Gets An Upgrade

• Does China Control Bitcoin? Ripple/XRP CEO Brad Garlinghouse: Absolutely!

• BITCOIN, ETHEREUM & XRP Exit Plan REVISITED

Other Notable Crypto YouTubers:

• 99Bitcoins
• Digital Asset Investor
• The Modern Investor
• Blockchain Backer
• Ivan on Tech
• Crypto Zombie
• Sheldon Evans
• Crypto Eri
• Crypto Capital Venture
• DustyBC Crypto News
• Bitcoin for Beginners

- Crypto Crew University
- Crypto Tips
- Alex Cobb
- Crypto Love
- Kevin Cage
- Crypto Jebb
- Thinking Crypto
- Digital Assets Daily
- Chico Crypto
- The Bearable Bull
- Hashoshi

Twitter

Before investing in cryptocurrency, I was turned off from the idea of Twitter. I thought it was a silly platform where users use it as a public diary for all their problems, which part of the platform is, however, following the right accounts allows your dashboard to be a sea of information. Creating an account specifically for crypto will flood out all the nonsense to zoom into business, economics, technical analysis, crypto news and the financial sector, which is very helpful to stay up to date. Depending on which cryptos you invest in, it would be a good idea to follow the core management team on Twitter and also follow the hashtags of your investments to retain the best information that caters to your portfolio.

Another good thing to do is to sign up for the alerts to your favourite Twitter accounts so whenever a new post gets tweeted, you'll get notifications on your phone if you have the app downloaded. This is great if you're a busy go-getter who doesn't have too much time to do research, so reading the headlines from the notifications can allow you to still keep up-to-date on the go. Below are my go-to Twitter accounts that I recommend following, besides myself, of course *wink wink* @FinancialVixen.

Prominent Crypto, Financial and Economic Figures:

- Raoul Pal - @RaoulGMI
- CZ Binance - @cz_binance
- Pomp - @APompliano
- Tim Draper - @TimDraper
- Christine Lagarde - @Lagarde
- Mark Cuban - @mcuban
- Therealkiyosaki - @theRealKiyosaki
- Michael Saylor - @michael_saylor
- Tyler Winklevoss - @tyler
- Cameron Winklevoss - @cameron
- David Gokhshtein - @davidgokhshtein
- Julia Chatterley - @jchatterleyCNN
- Laura Shin - @laurashin

Crypto Social Media Influencers:

- Kevin Cage - @Kevin_Cage_
- Working Money - @WorkingMoneyCH
- CryptoWhale - @CryptoWhale
- Layah Heilpern - @LayahHeilpern
- Crypto Eri - @sentosumosaba
- Sheldon Evans - @Sheldon_Evans
- Ivan on Tech - @IvanOnTech
- XRPcryptowolf - @XRPcryptowolf
- The Modern Investor - @ModernInvest
- Digital Assets Daily - @AssetsDaily
- Thinking Crypto - @ThinkingCrypto1
- Altcoin Daily - @AltcoinDailyio
- Digital Asset News - @NewsAsset
- Secrets - @SecretsOfCrypto
- Digital Asset Investor - @digitalassetbuy

- Lark Davis - @TheCryptoLark
- Digital Perspectives - @BakkupBradley
- Girl Gone Crypto - @girlgone_crypto
- BankXRP - @BankXRP
- XRP Owl - @XRP_OWL
- The Wolf Of All Streets - @scottmelker

Prominent Crypto, Business, Monetary, Economic and Financial News Sources:

- Cointelegraph - @Cointelegraph
- CointelegraphMT - @CointelegraphZN
- CoinDesk - @CoinDesk
- CoinDesk Markets - @CoinDeskMarkets
- The Daily Hodl - @TheDailyHodl
- Real Vision - @RealVision
- Bloomberg Economics - @economics
- World Economic Forum - @wef
- Squawk Box - @SquawkCNBC
- Forbes Crypto - @ForbesCrypto
- Bloomberg Crypto - @crypto
- European Central Bank - @ecb
- The Economist - @TheEconomist
- IMF - @IMFNews

Crypto Influencers Technical Analysis Accounts:

- CRYPTOWZRD - @cryptoWZRD_
- CryptoYoda - @CryptoYoda1338
- DonAlt - @CryptoDonAlt
- Credible Crypto - @CredibleCrypto
- Peter Brandt - @PeterLBrandt
- Cred - @CryptoCred
- TheCryptoSniper - @TheCryptoSniper

- Luke Martin - @VentureCoinist
- 360Trader - @360_trader
- Cryptic Crypto - @Crypto_Dior
- Dark Defender - @DefendDark
- Bearybullish - @bearybullish1

Reddit

Reddit.com is a platform where users join various groups (subreddits) ranging from any topic whether its science, sports, music or even cryptocurrency for instance. Users posts within the subreddit are up voted or down voted and for every vote on a post or comment, whether good or bad, increases or decreases a user's karma points. These karma points add credibility to users' accounts which gain a lot of respect within the Reddit community and users can also be rewarded Reddit's own digital "coin" for their respected content.

Many groups tend to have an automated moderator that restricts content from being posted by users who haven't been on the platform long enough or if an account doesn't have a specific amount of karma points. This, however, doesn't restrict users from still reading through the content posted within groups, but rather creates a trusted online community to flood your dashboard with interesting content.

r/cryptocurrency - The main source for cryptocurrency on the platform for discussions, news, technical analysis and entertaining content.

r/bitcoin - Main source of information on the platform for all your Bitcoin needs. It also contains an informative list of links on the side to help wrap your head around the coin if you're a beginner.

r/bitcoinbeginners - A safe and inviting group for beginners to ease into the space. You can post questions within the group and most likely get a quick and helpful reply.

r/crypto_currency_news - This useful subreddit has strict rules for users to follow to keep the content consistent with relevant information. Content must have a link to a credible site or else it will get banned and Facebook or Twitter posts are prohibited.

r/XRP - Subreddit for all updates on XRP which also contains a helpful list of resources to help beginners understand and invest in XRP.

r/cryptomarkets - One of the more serious subreddits specifically for trading cryptocurrency. The information includes technical analysis and AMA (ask me anything) features that have reputable professionals within the sector answering investors questions in one thread.

r/ethtrader - Largest cryptocurrency subreddit specifically for Ethereum and any information that does not relate to Ethereum gets banned.

TradingView

Aside from the misleading name, Trading View is not a trading exchange, but rather a portal for all trading markets where you can have access to charts and technical analysis. It is also a network where other investors come together to share their analysis, discuss price action, news and personal opinions within the various sectors. There is also an insightful 'fundamentals dial' when searching for a company or crypto that indicates with a needle if a stock or crypto is a "strong sell, sell, neutral, buy or strong buy." The site is free to join but if you decide to upgrade your plan, you can get $30 for free by using the link below:

https://bit.ly/3vtds3c

Quora

Quora.com is a brilliant platform where users ask questions on any topic and other users respond by posting a credible source of information or simply reply with their personal opinion. If you have any questions within the crypto community, chances are someone else was wondering about the same thing and has already posted a question on the site, which would most likely have a chain of responses attached. If you want a quick answer to any troubling questions you may have, Quora is the perfect platform.

8

Investment Strategies

"By failing to prepare you are preparing to fail."

- Benjamin Franklin

Befoe diving into the wonderful world of cryptocurrency, you need to determine what kind of investor you will be by having an investment strategy. This will allow you to have structure with your investments and is a helpful way of staying focused by not allowing your emotions to get the best of you within an extremely volatile market.

The three common methods of investing are by day trading, swing trading and long-term investing. Day trading is when a person buys a crypto or a stock to move in and out of the market for a short period of time, typically a day, while watching the fluctuations of the price meticulously to make a quick short-term profit. Swing trading is when an investor attempts to hold an asset for a few days to several weeks in hopes of gaining profit in a short-to-medium time frame. The most favourable strategy is by investing on a long-term basis by understanding the long-term vision of a crypto. By having a long-term mentality, investors buy and hold a digital asset hoping that the price will increase over a long duration of time, typically longer than a year, to then sell their position at a higher price. Although day trading is regarded as a way to get rich quick, there are a handful of risks involved that people tend to not focus on when greed takes the driver's seat. There are various ways of making money within the crypto sector, but having a long-term strategy is by far the safer option for beginners – especially those who have a full-time job and do not want to make their investments their full-time priority.

As nerve-wracking as it is to dive into the market at first, altcoinfantasy.com is a free trading simulation that offers fake money with real-time price fluctuations, which is great to practice buying in and out of digital assets in a risk free environment. The platform is easy to use, features the main cryptocurrencies within the sector, gives an explanation of each crypto and also includes links to news articles. Additionally, there is a Learning Academy on the platform that explains how to trade and includes an introduction into what blockchain technology is. If you're nervous about investing in cryptocurrency, then Altcoin Fantasy would be a good place to develop your skills to gain confidence for when you finally decide to take the leap of faith into the actual market.

While day trading may seem alluring, an interesting study carried out by Berkeley University, reported that a groundbreaking 80% of day traders lose money annually and "more than 75% of all day traders quit within two years." Trying to time the market can be like catching a falling knife, so if you are considering day trading, it is strongly urged for those ballsy enough to take professional courses, learn how to do technical analysis, learn trade setups and exit plans before taking the plunge. Since this book is an introductory guide into the sector, this chapter will focus on long-term strategies. Although speculation is a massive part of the crypto market, using long-term strategies can help shape an investor's mindset and reduce risk within a very volatile market to control your flow of money. The two strategies discussed will be lump sum investing and dollar cost averaging.

Lump Sum Investing

Lump sum investing is when someone enters a market using their money to buy a position all at once, hoping that the price increases at a later date to sell at a higher price. Let's say you saved £1000 and you want to invest in Bitcoin. A lump sum investment would mean that you take the full £1000 and buy £1000 worth at that moment, hoping for dear life that the price goes up over a long period of time to then sell at a higher price. Although there are no guarantees, if you look at a cryptos lifetime chart on an exchange, you will see over the span of a few years if there has been an incline or decline.

Lump sum investing tends to be the more rewarding method of long-term investing; however, the entire investment is exposed to the market. You can profit more naturally when the market price is good, but it also exposes you to the potential of declining market prices.

The obvious drawback of lump sum investing is that you place all your money at risk, so you need to carefully pick your investment portfolio, while keeping your nerves intact during critical times. A lot of this is down to one's own mindset and financial conditions as well. If the market dips, would you mentally be prepared to power through?

Dollar Cost Averaging (DCA)

Due to a lot of beginner investors chasing the hype and not timing the market accordingly, when prices drop, nerves can often cloud judgment by leading one to panic sell. One of the best ways to avoid this scenario is for investors to use the 'dollar cost average' strategy.

Dollar cost averaging (DCA) is a tactic to invest a consistent amount of money in regular intervals whether it be weekly, biweekly or monthly etc., regardless of the flow of the market. If you had £1000 to invest and you wanted to invest in Bitcoin for instance, you can split the £1000 in equal parts to invest an equal fraction on the 1st of every month on a long-term basis. If you don't have a lump sum of money and have factored in a certain amount of money every month after bills, rent and expenses have been factored out, the same investment strategy applies to invest the same amount of money over a period of time, regardless of what the market price is. Instead of trying to time the market, this strategy is used to methodically compound growth and essentially reduce risks to shudder off those investing nerves. The 'average' concept derives from the fact that whatever price the market is presently at, you are committed to investing capital for the same project. Price fluctuations vary from month to month, but doing this method expects the average price over a long period of time to be financially beneficial, which is statistically likely to do so.

Lastly, the advantage of dollar cost averaging is that it is a safer approach to reducing risk within such a volatile market, however, it's key to remember that the incremental gains will be slower and modest.

Long-Term Mentality

As a long-term investor, you need to be confident that the investments you're making have a promising future over the next few years. Even if you don't stay up-to-date regularly with news, doing proper research to understand the long-term growth, partnerships, goals and value of the cryptos you invest in, will ultimately help control your emotions when the market is in red. Typically in situations like this, unprepared investors let their emotions cloud their judgement, which can lead to a downward spiral of regret and fury. Thinking long-term trains your mind through the dips of the market – you'll be so confident of the future plans that would boost the price, the thought of selling won't even phase you.

Skeptics tend to compare investing to gambling, but it's only gambling if you don't put effort into building a strategy and doing research to have more control over your money. Realistically, successful investors train their mind to power through the short-term pain, to later come out on top with long-term gains. After creating an investment strategy and training your mind to think long-term, the next step to controlling your investments is to create an exit plan.

Exit Plan

Having an exit strategy for every investment you make is crucial for preparing how the market will sway. A strategy set in stone will allow you to be smart with your money, otherwise you'll be gambling – no different than if you were at a casino. If you prefer to play the market by gambling then fair play to you, but if you want to make the most of your investments, having a strategy to follow will be very beneficial. Some people take the risk by not planning ahead, hoping to sell whenever the price reaches an all-time high. However, if this plan turns south and the crypto reaches an all-time low, then this is where fear and emotions get the best of investors and many panic sell – ultimately leading to a dent in their portfolio.

Buy low and sell high – how hard could that be right? As discussed within chapter 2, the Bitcoin halving event is a pivotal way to determine the sway of the crypto market, whether we will be in a bear (declining) or bull (inclining) market. A helpful indication of when the market enters a bull market is when there is an upward trend of 20% for the whole market following a previous decline, and the same concept applies for a 20% downward trend to enter a bear market.

One of the best ways to help strategise your entry and exit strategy within the market is to think of a bear market as the perfect buying opportunity, whereas bull markets are key for gaining profits by selling. This mindset can help strategise your entry and exit points, while also factoring in the halving event for Bitcoin. This can skillfully guide you on how to gauge where the direction of the market will go.

A previous indication that was helpful for guessing how the market will sway is by calculating roughly 500 days for a bull market cycle within the crypto space. By taking this into consideration and calculating 500 days after the May 11th, 2020 halving event would position September 23rd, 2021 for when the market could *potentially* start to decline. Although this is not a definite date for when the market will start to tank since previous patterns can change, keeping this date and calculation in mind could be helpful when creating an exit or entry strategy. It is also important to note that the 2021 bull market is different to previous years due to institutional interests and the new flood of mass attention. For this reason, many analysts estimate that the 2021 bull market *could* last longer than previous years and slightly bleed into 2022.

Although timing the market is like trying to catch a falling knife, setting price targets to sell a certain percentage of your holdings when the price hits your forecasted targets is a key way of creating an exit strategy. This will give you the structure you need to put your mind at ease within such a volatile market. As strenuous as it may seem, keeping your plan simple is key;

below are hypothetical targets created to showcase an *example* of various exit strategies.

XRP Exit Strategy (Example 1)

Expected Target in $	Converted Target to £	6% of £ Target	Est. Selling Range	% To Sell
$10.00	£7.05	£6.62	£6.62 - £7.05	5%
$25.00	£17.63	£16.57	£16.57 - £17.63	5%
$50.00	£35.26	£33.14	£33.14 - £35.26	10%
$100.00	£70.53	£66.30	£66.30 - £70.53	15%
$250.00	£176.62	£165.74	£165.74 - £176.62	20%
$500.00	£352.64	£331.48	£331.48 - £352.64	20%

XRP Exit Strategy (Example 2)

Expected Target in $	Converted Target to £	6% of £ Target	Est. Selling Range	% To Sell
$10.00	£7.05	£6.62	£6.62 - £7.05	5%
$50.00	£35.26	£33.14	£33.14 - £35.26	10%
$250.00	£176.62	£165.74	£165.74 - £176.62	20%
$500.00	£352.64	£331.48	£331.48 - £352.64	20%
$1000.00	£705.28	£662.96	£662.96 - £705.28	25%

The far-left column contains the anticipated price targets in USD within the next few years – these are not guaranteed, but rather based on personal expectations. To the right of the first column are the price targets converted from USD to GBP due to my main fiat money being GBP. This does not mean that if GBP is not your main currency that this restricts you, but you can simply base your targeted price off from the main target. It is, however, not recommended to base your selling points on the initial expected target due to the herd mentality that many other investors will try to do the same. What you want to do is to try and sell as high as you can before the mob does the same, ultimately leading the price to drop. This is why 6% of the expected target was calculated, which also features a range of prices to have a flexible window. Finally, the selling percentage chosen is to gradually allow more growth while also claiming profits.

Another notable exit strategy many investors choose to follow is when you double your investment, to sell half which leaves only your profits in the market. This can be a "safer" approach due to only playing with your profits, which can be considered as money you've already lost.

In terms of selling a position, many investors choose to keep their wealth tied into cryptocurrency by converting to a 'stablecoin' to get away from the volatility of the market. If you were to sell £1000 worth of Cardano for instance, instead of converting it to your local fiat money to then store it in a bank account, you can simply convert it to a stablecoin such as Coinbase (CBDC), Paxos Standard (PAX), Tether (USDT), Binance (BGBP) or (BUSD) to keep the value of £1000 stable within a cryptocurrency. Many investors choose to do this to then store their wealth on a hardware wallet for safe keeping. This method is not for everyone as it depends on your own circumstances to fit your own personal needs.

If any of the above strategies don't pique your interest, then you can simply sell whenever you feel is best for you. There are no set rules – to each their own – but the above acts as a guideline to effectively gain profits, while strategically navigating through the sways of the markets. Depending on how much money you have invested and how long you want to remain in the market, entry and exit strategies vary depending on each investor's research, confidence and emotional attachment to the market. Although these methods may not be everyone's cup of tea, it is still an effective tactic to know to start brewing strategies and to have a structured plan.

9

Be Smart and Not a Target

"Privacy is power.
What people don't know,
they can't ruin."

- Anonymous

111

W hen it comes to investing in cryptocurrency, you need to take every precaution you can to keep your money safe. If you don't take care of your money, no one will do it for you and you put a target on your back by not being cautious.

The first step to being safe is to make sure that your phone and computer requires a strong password for entry. God forbid you lose your phone or laptop and the curious George who found your belongings snoops around and stumbles upon your exchanges' app. You instantly put yourself at risk so that the curious George can rinse you dry of your money. Which brings me to my second point – create a 2-step authentication for your exchanges' app and email account.

It is recommended to create a new email address specifically for anything related to crypto. Refrain from using your real name and don't add your phone number in the signature since hackers can use phone numbers to their advantage. This email should then be the only email used to sign into the exchanges or platforms you are a part of. By ditching your Gmail or Hotmail account for an end-to-end email service from protonmail.com, you can encrypt your emails for extra security. This free service allows a system of communication that only the sender and the receiver can read the messages. You can even go the extra mile to keep your online activity private by subscribing for ProtonVPN that encrypts your internet connection for an extra layer of protection. Selecting this option allows users activity or passwords to not get logged into the system, which means your data will remain safe.

When it comes to creating a password for any exchange, platform or email service, it is crucial to have at least a 16-character password that includes special characters, numbers, uppercase and lowercase letters. By taking these simplified precautions and managing your privacy, you will create a difficult shield for hackers to break through. However, the most critical piece of advice I can give is that if you follow all these steps but regret to keep your passwords offline or completely off your devices, you ultimately create the biggest target on your back. All passwords must not be saved on any browser, document, password saver or anywhere on your computer, usb or hard drive for that matter. Passwords must remain offline – write it down and put it in a lockable safe, special hiding spot, make multiple copies to spread throughout your home, tattoo it (just kidding) or even laminate it. You should take every precaution to not link any passwords to your phone or computer as this will ultimately leave you wearing camouflage on the battlefield.

Cryptocurrency Scams

The next phase of being safe within the crypto space is recognising a scam when it looks you in the eye. As tempting as it can be, the golden rule is to always think that if something seems too good to be true, then it's most likely a scam. If you're a risk taker then go for it, but it will most likely be your funeral in the end.

As intriguing as the crypto market is due to the potential of receiving a high return on investment, the sector unfortunately comes with people who try to prey on the weak. One of the most infamous crypto scams comes from the "Crypto Queen" Dr. Ruja Ignatova, who has yet to be put behind bars for her devious four-billion-dollar scheme. The tragically interesting story is featured as a podcast by the BBC called, "The Missing Cryptoqueen" and contains 8 episodes of Dr. Ruja's rise of creating a fake cryptocurrency.

The 'OneCoin' scam is essentially a multi-level pyramid scheme selling copyrighted educational packages. Unlike real cryptocurrencies, where you can buy and sell directly on various exchanges, 'OneCoin' was only rewarded to investors who initially spent £1000 - £150,000 on various packages directly on the OneCoin platform and nowhere else. Red flag number one. Each package had a certain amount of 'OneCoin' attached as a reward, however, investors couldn't even convert their 'OneCoin' into real fiat money. Red flag number two. The only real way of essentially making fiat money was to sell these packages and to convince others to hop on board and sell the packages as a team to profit off of each other's sales. Red flag number three.

Imagine a day spent in a stadium with a sea of eager people wanting to make a difference in their lives. Energising music is blasting to energise the crowd along with motivational speeches that confidently claimed OneCoin would overtake Bitcoin. The ambiance alone made victims fall into the spell cast by ringleader Dr. Ruja Ignatova. She fed off the vulnerable and created an illusion where, "OneCoin is more of a coin – it's a family and a vision."

She manipulated her followers to sell packages in which many sold their homes, cars and even took out loans to "invest" in the false hopes and dreams of what the fake coin could have brought. With secret hand symbols and urging followers to speak ill towards anyone who goes against the OneCoin vision, correlated to the foundation of what a cult is. This ultimately created a sophisticated pyramid scheme with a cult following.

The ironic flaw with OneCoin was the confident claim that it would be the coin to overtake Bitcoin, yet it lacked the fundamental elements of what makes Bitcoin so strong – blockchain technology and the scarcity of coins. OneCoin did not have its own blockchain and coins would be pumped out of thin air – red flag number four. What was even more shocking was the fact that Dr. Ruja spoon fed lies that inflation at OneCoin was a good move to get more people on board. Reality check: inflation is never good. As a result, her followers blindly cheered her on because they thought the value of the coins they possessed only on the OneCoin website would double in value.

The story is interesting nonetheless, but a tragedy for the many who fell as a victim. The importance of this scam showcases the negligence many investors had by being blindsided of the illusion of potential fortune. The most crucial thing an investor can do for themselves is to do research, otherwise you're just gambling with your money. The heart-wrenching part of the BBC's podcast is listening to victims reminisce on their OneCoin experience who spent thousands without even knowing what blockchain technology is and how it works. They simply hopped on board the FOMO (Fear of Missing Out) train without setting time aside to learn the basics, which could have triggered a red flag had they done so. Through a web of lies spun by the sophisticated pyramid schemes, many lessons can be learned from this scam:

- To feel safer with your investments, double check that the crypto you invest in is available on other exchanges. OneCoin only existed on its own website.

- Do research before investing into a crypto to confirm if you're able to convert that crypto into fiat money. If not, that's a redflag.

- Invest in cryptos that appear in the top 20 on coinmarketcap.com for more credibility.

- Any crypto incentive given after making a purchase for a package or any sort of reward should be a red flag.

- The only fees you should pay when dealing with crypto are the exchanges' buying and selling fees directly.

- Research the team involved in the crypto you are investing in. Dr. Ruja had a criminal past before OneCoin and a simple Google search would have brought her past actions into light to trigger a red flag.

- Always ensure that the URL of web pages has the 's' in 'httpS' since many scams include only 'http'.

The troubling part of the OneCoin scam is the fact that the pyramid scheme is still active and squeezing people dry of their hard-earned money. Rumour has it that Dr. Ruja has undergone a tremendous amount of plastic surgery and has dyed her hair blonde to make herself unrecognisable. With Ignatova's devious ties to the mob and her pockets that run deep, only time will tell if she continues to live her life on the run or if she will be joining her brother behind bars. For a deeper perspective on the scam and of Dr. Ruja Ignatova, The Missing Cryptoqueen is a wonderful glimpse into the crooked story for those who get a thrill from true crime stories. The podcast can be found on Apple podcasts or directly on the BBCs' website.

Along with the OneCoin scheme are two clever scams that are currently in circulation which involve Elon Musk and Jeff Bezos. When casually falling down the rabbit hole of watching Dragons' Den and Shark Tank clips on YouTube at 3:00 AM, I found myself getting targeted ads from SpaceX for a Bitcoin giveaway. I was intrigued so I clicked on the video and was redirected on YouTube to a SpaceX channel with Elon Musk giving a lecture. On the same stream, a box of text was over the video with instructions on how to claim free Bitcoin.

The text stated that if you transferred a certain amount of Bitcoin from your wallet to the stated address, then their backend system would magically convert your transferred amount into a doubled figure back into your wallet. The channel had over 200k subscribers, had a name similar to the real SpaceX channel and had a live broadcast which made it seem like the real deal. After a simple Google search and browsing on Musk's social media, it was apparent that Musk had absolutely no involvement whatsoever and many people were suckered into sending Bitcoin without receiving anything in return. Many prominent figures such as Richard Branson, Jeff Bezos and even Ethereum founder Vitalik Buterin, have been looped into these schemes to try and add a credible name to the scam.

In addition, 2020 surfaced a lot of sophisticated scams where 130 high-profile Twitter accounts got hacked, which made it seem that prominent figures such as Barack Obama, Joe Biden, Elon Musk and Bill Gates were giving away free cryptocurrency from verified accounts if people sent money to a certain address. Unfortunately, since it was their actual account, many people fell as a victim to this £150 million scam. However, it teaches the valuable lesson to always dig a bit deeper than the surface for any information that is presented.

Lastly, the most common and cringeworthy scams are amongst the comments section across various social media platforms. There are a swarm of impersonators of crypto influencers or 'fund managers', that comment with a sappy success story that offers a WhatsApp number or an email to contact for financial advice. Whenever you see a number or an email in the comments section, just simply ignore it and carry on with your day.

As cryptocurrency becomes more popular, more scams will flourish to try and target the weak. If something seems too good to be true, then chances are that it is too good and we must all fight the temptation to be suckered into a hackers scam and take personal accountability. Those who are cautious and treat everything as a scam until proven otherwise, will be the investors who excel in the sector. Contrarily, you will fall as a victim drowning in a pit of regret if you're not cautious.

Be smart and not a target.

10

Mistakes Investors Make

"If you fail to plan, you are planning to fail!"

- Benjamin Franklin

One of the best ways to learn about a new subject is to learn from the mistakes of those who have succeeded in any field. A lot of people are scared from making mistakes and are blindsided at the fact that these troubling moments are the most powerful moments for a lesson to be learned to essentially grow. This chapter is a collection of the most common mistakes to give you the guidance to confidently take the leap of faith into a new sector. Strengthening on the below points will ultimately allow you to practice self-discipline, learn risk management and self-liability.

1. No matter what sector an investor is in, the number one rule of investing is:

DO NOT INVEST MORE THAN YOU'RE WILLING TO LOSE!

The above cannot be expressed enough and is straight to the point that hopefully does not need any further explanation. Do not let greed get the best of your judgment.

2. Don't rush into the market without knowing the basics of the sector and the digital assets that you are investing in.

Pop quiz: If you can't answer the basic questions below before diving into the crypto market, then you need to take a halt on investing and do more research.

- What are the problems the project you are invested in is trying to solve?

- What is blockchain technology?

- Who are the core team members and are they credible?

- What are the long-term goals of the crypto?

- What partnerships do the crypto's have?

- What is the competition doing?

- What are the potential risks and rewards?

- Is the crypto within the top 20 coins on coinmarketcap.com to make the project more credible?

3. Investors need to have an exit plan for each investment.

Depending on the projects you invest in, the entry and exit strategy should differ from coin to coin. Setting up guidelines to follow will help you have a clear strategy for when the markets turn sour. The key to success is to have a plan and no matter what happens, stick to that plan.

4. Don't put your eggs in one basket, but also make sure not to over diversify your portfolio.

Due to the high volatility in the crypto market, holding more than one asset helps minimise risk. However, some investors make the mistake of holding too many assets where it becomes too overwhelming to keep up with the evolving advancements for each project.

It is key to remember that every investors' strategy is different based on their own financial and life circumstances. Investor A might be able to juggle 10-15 assets due to their full concentration throughout the day being tied to the sector. Whereas investor B could work a 9-5 job, maybe have a family and can only research the sector on their way to work. Investor B can comfortably stay up-to-date with 1-3 assets, for instance, while investor A has more time to focus on his investments, which gives him the confidence to hold a diverse portfolio. Whatever your situation is, you need to be confident that you are not following the investment strategy of someone who is in a completely different situation than yourself. Realise that investing in one asset creates a lot more risk but holding too many assets can be detrimental to achieving your long-term goals. Don't bite more than you're willing to chew.

5. Come to terms that everyone including yourself will lose money every now and again.

Losing money in any sector is normal and you need to be strong minded by being in such a volatile market to power through. One day the market could be up 60% and another day it can be down by 40%. You need to be mentally prepared to accept the fluctuations of how the market sways and if it makes you nervous then maybe you need to rethink your position.

6. Don't let your emotions dictate your trades.

The lawsuit against Ripple is a perfect example of investors letting their emotions get the best of them to panic sell. Investors go on a roller coaster ride of emotions where fear, frustration, anxiety, excitement, hope and greed will challenge you to your very core. The crypto sector is extremely volatile and it's exhilarating to receive high returns but can be deadly for the weak minded when the market dips, causing some investors to panic sell. You 100% need to have tough skin to make it out on the other side with a smile on your face. Otherwise, you will fall victim to your emotional demons by being unprepared and cast under the spell of fear and greed which can cloud any sense of logic. This is why doing your long-term due diligence will help you paint a clear path for the projects you're invested in to help you through the low hurdles.

Viewing market dips as a good buying opportunity as if there is a sale at your favourite store is also key to succeeding. This way of thinking gives a contrarian perspective by strategically accumulating more crypto to later sell at a higher price. Dips, crashes and bear markets are inevitable and is brutal, but it's how you react in these moments that are crucial. Short term pain, for long term gain.

7. Understand what the fear of missing out is and don't chase the pumps.

What goes up will come back down, so just be patient and wait for the dips to buy in.

8. Don't fall victim to scams!

Remember that if an opportunity pops up to make a quick return that sounds too good to be true, it's probably a scam. Also, never send money before researching where it is going first.

9. Research the good, the bad and the ugly.

Along with absorbing bullish information pertaining to the crypto(s) you're invested in, it is important to research into the negative as well. This allows you to have a complete understanding of your investments from different angles which gives you a contrarian perception to not always follow the herd.

10. Take every precaution you can to be safe within the sector.

Write your passwords down, make copies and hide it. Get a hardware wallet to store your cryptocurrency offline to avoid hacks and tears. If you send crypto to someone, double, triple and quadruple check the address you are sending crypto to because if one character is incorrect, there goes your money without the ability to claim it back. Don't rush decisions and take your time to be safe.

11. Beginners should stick to long-term investments when they first enter the market.

Mining, leveraging and day trading for instance, is very complex for a beginner to dive into the market straight away without the proper training. Those who refuse to do so will most likely lose money out of negligence. The less trades made is usually more profitable since trying to time the market is like trying to catch a falling knife. Buying and selling fees on exchanges can also eat into profits which add up over time. Without knowing, some investors' fees end up higher than profits when keeping a close eye on numbers slips under the radar. Statistically, buying and holding an asset for a long period of time reduces your chances of making poor decisions. Holding long-term also lowers your tax liabilities if held for longer than a year.

12. Pay your taxes!

Regardless of if cryptocurrency is decentralised or not, if you live in a country that recognises cryptocurrency as a legal asset, you must pay capital gains tax. If not, you put yourself at risk of paying the repercussions out of neglect.

13. Stick to what you know.

Regardless of any investment, you must not invest in cryptocurrencies just for the sake of investing because someone you know or look up to invests in it.

14. In order to buy any crypto, you do not need to buy the full price listed but can buy a fraction of the listed price.

This was annoyingly the first mistake I made when I entered the market. I was waking up between 3:00 - 5:00 AM to look at my phone to check the prices of Bitcoin like a hopscotch game trying to carefully time myself into the market. I would have saved a lot of hassle and sleep if I knew this before investing.

15. Transactions cannot be reversed.

If you were to send money using your bank account and you realised that you sent it to the wrong person, you could easily call your bank and have the transaction cancelled. This is not the case with crypto as once a transaction is made, you cannot recoup it. This is crucial to why always double checking the addresses you are sending crypto to is correct.

16. Do not withdraw your crypto, convert it to fiat and store it into a savings account with a bank.

There are a handful of crypto platforms that offer higher interest rates than any bank would dare to offer if you lend your crypto. The most common sites are listed below:

- KuCoin - https://bit.ly/3yeImxY
- Celsius.network
- Blockfi.com
- Binance - https://bit.ly/3fjknov
- Abra.com

17. "Be fearful when others are greedy and greedy when others are fearful" - Warren Buffet.

Final Thoughts

Although a few of the points above may be old news for some, there are still a lot of stubborn people who tend to not do what they know they have to do. If you're smirking right now, then it means you're probably one of the guilty ones who can relate to this statement ever so much. It's a common yet self-destructive trait many possess, but when it comes to investing, the tenacious habit of being stubborn needs to be swallowed up or else it may sabotage your investments.

Some investors even go the extra mile to track their mistakes in a notebook to use as a learning curve of how to tackle their mistakes differently. Was the trade based on panic selling? Did you buy an asset due to the fear of missing out? These are the kinds of questions, for example, that can be applied when trying to analyse investment patterns head on. Although this method is not for everyone, it is an additional strategy for those who would like to track their process and progress because it can definitely help structure future trades.

Mistakes will be made along the way but learning to embrace the mistakes to then grow from them will be the ultimate blessing in disguise.

11

What to Do When the Taxman Cometh?

"Capital gains tax is theft!"

- Common Phrase Amongst Investors

Many investors have very strong opinions based on the quote on the previous page. Why should we have to pay a large percentage of our profits to the government!? I get that it is for emergency services etc., which is a blessing, but it is absolutely ludicrous that some countries have 50% capital gains tax that squeezes you dry for your hard-earned profits. The reality is that as investors we have to annoyingly comply with the law or else there will be several repercussions for our ignorance. Although there are many crypto friendly countries, the regulations differ in every country depending on where you live. Below is a quick overview as of 2020 of the leading countries that have regarded cryptocurrency as a legal asset and some of the countries that have placed a ban.

Leading Crypto-Friendly Countries

United States	Canada	United Kingdom
Switzerland	Hong Kong	Germany
The Netherlands	Singapore	Malta
Japan	Georgia	Belarus
Ukraine	Lithuania	Gibraltar
Estonia	Bermuda	Slovenia
Australia	New Zealand	

Countries that Have Banned Cryptocurrency

Afghanistan	Pakistan	Algeria
Bolivia	Bangladesh	Saudi Arabia
Vietnam	Qatar	Vanuatu
The Republic of Macedonia	Russia	Nepal
Zambia	Morocco	Ecuador
Egypt	Samoa	China
Nigeria	India	

Although several countries were not listed above, many regions still remain in legal limbo due to various governments not creating a legal guideline for cryptocurrency. Depending on the country, the ban on digital assets may not scare many away since crypto has proven to be an essential alternative against the corrupt systems in power. The ability to purchase and trade cryptocurrency is accessible to anyone with an internet connection and is ultimately seen as a glimpse of hope against governments' venal fiat money and economic challenges.

Although cryptocurrency is decentralised, a lot of people assume that we don't have to pay tax, which is a big fat myth. If you want to take those odds then by all means do so at your own risk, but if you're an investor in a country that has deemed cryptocurrency as a legal asset, then it is highly recommended that you obey the regulations set by the government of the country you reside. In the UK, for instance, the capital gains tax is more flexible than other countries by only having to pay taxes after hitting £12,300 of profit made, whereas in Canada 50% of gains is treacherously taxable regardless of your profits.

Depending on the country, the taxable accounts may be on every trade made, whilst other countries have regulations in place where holding an asset longer than a year allows taxes to be lower. This is not for every country, but simply used as an example to showcase the various ways that the government can tax your crypto gains. This is why it is recommended to get a professional crypto savvy accountant to handle your taxes to answer any uneasy questions.

As stressful as taxes can be, there are a lot of useful tools and websites to specifically help with the admin process. Exchanges usually have a feature on the website where you can download a document that showcases a full history of all of your transactions. After merging all trades from different exchanges into one document, it can be uploaded onto websites that help with the admin process.

Recap is a great website within the UK to import trades and the software crunches the numbers needed for HMRC to reduce the manual admin and bookkeeping. The site has a free option if you have less than 100 trades which is great if you don't trade a lot, but after 1000 trades, it's £120 per year, £240 for 5000 trades per year and then £400 for 25,000 trades per year. Using the promo link below will allow you to get 20% off:

https://bit.ly/3k5U9rL

Additional promo code: 4e8158848cea

Another great site that I found extremely useful was Tax Scout. I was initially drawn to the site because it had a built in Capital Gains Tax calculator for the UK where you can simply put your annual salary and how much profit you want to take from your investments. The site then automatically calculates the tax and showcases the breakdown in a matter of seconds. After snooping around on the site, I then realised that Tax Scout can actually assign you an accountant to file your assessment. They do all the admin that nobody wants to do for "£119 all in". I wish I found this site a lot sooner, but better late than never. Using the promo link below will allows you to get 10% off your first tax return:

https://bit.ly/3wWG0Tu

If you're not in the UK, additional sites such as Crypto Trader offer the same ease of bookkeeping within the US and Australia and the below link will also offer a 10% discount:

https://bit.ly/37wOLIW

Promo code: CRYPTOTAX10

If you're currently residing within another country, a simple Google search will suffice if you need a similar site as the ones mentioned above. For further information pertaining to the taxation laws in the country you reside in, please make sure to visit your government's official website. It is imperative to do your own due diligence on capital gains tax specifically in regard to the cryptocurrency laws within your country before you invest to avoid any uncertainty or penalties.

12

Coinspiracies

"First they ignore you,
then they laugh at you,
then they fight you,
then you win."

– Anonymous (Not Gandhi as many believe)

N ow this is the part of the book where the information gets juicy yet controversial. Some may find conspiracy theories relating to crypto intriguing and others will find it completely ludicrous. Either way, there are three thought-provoking conspiracies that are fun to debate in which a small percentage of people within the sector are aware of. I am not stating that the three are true nor false, but merely presenting these intriguing theories for you to make a decision for yourself or to spark interest that would make you want to do further research. If you're the kind of person who can't take conspiracy theories seriously, then you may want to skip this chapter entirely, but if you're interested in conspiracies that can potentially make you money, then carry on reading.

The Simpsons

It may be of surprise to many, but *one* of the most mathematically sophisticated television shows in the history of prime time broadcasting is The Simpsons. This is simply due to the fact that a lot of the writers on the show possess a masters' degree in mathematics from Harvard, but chose to follow their creative writing passion. However, they still express their love for numbers by sneakily ingraining complex mathematics within some of the episodes.

When Simon Singh was doing research for his book, *The Simpsons and Their Mathematical Secrets*, the best-selling author hung out with the shows' main writers for research and recalled his experience in an interview with The Guardian. One particular head scratching moment he mentioned was when the writers discussed their interest in incorporating "freeze-frame gags" within the episodes.

> *"Freeze-frame gags are visual quips that fly unnoticed during the normal course of viewing, but which become more obvious when the programme is paused. The writers relished the notion of the freeze-frame gag, because*

> *it enabled them to increase the comedic density. The mathematicians on the show were doubly keen because freeze-frame gags also gave them the opportunity to introduce obscure references that rewarded the hard-core number nerds."*

A mind-boggling freeze-frame gag appeared in the 1998 episode titled, 'The Wizard of Evergreen Terrace,' where Homer attempted to be an inventor. In one of the scenes, he scribbled on a blackboard which quickly popped up on the screen unnoticeable by a quick glance, yet once paused, you can see the scribble. It was the mass of the Higgs Boson (aka the God particle), 14 years before Peter Higgs and François Englert discovered it and won the Nobel Prize for doing so.

The Simpsons have been notorious for planned programming from stating the exact scores of the Super Bowl, predicting Trumps' presidency ahead of his public campaign, knowing the U.S. will beat Sweden in curling at the Olympics, to even recreating the plot twist for the finale of Game of Thrones. These episodes were all years in advance of the actual events, which is perplexing to say the least. A full list of eerie coincidences keeps piling up since the inception of the show, so it was only a natural reaction to get excited when finding out that a full episode released in February 2020 revolved around cryptocurrency – Season 31, episode 13. Regardless of if you are familiar with The Simpsons or not, the basis of the episode is easy to understand without the need of watching previous episodes.

The summary of the episode is that the scientist Professor Frink developed a cryptocurrency called Frinkcoin that drove him to become the richest person in Springfield. This bumped Mr. Burns into second place for the richest person in town, which threw him into a state of fury. Burning with a passion to sabotage Frinkcoin, Mr. Burns hired a few mathematicians to try and figure out how to dethrone Frinkcoin as the dominant coin by creating a new cryptocurrency called Burns Coin. Confused by what cryptocurrency is, Frink showed Lisa a video of Jim Parsons (who played Sheldon Cooper in Big Bang Theory) to help explain with a catchy Schoolhouse Rock-esque jingle deeming cryptocurrency as, "cash of the future." To watch this clip, a simple YouTube search with "Jim Parsons explains cryptocurrency" will pop up.

The jingle is sung by an animated book that represents a ledger and interestingly enough, the explanation given is not a broad description of what cryptocurrency is as a whole. Instead, the song craftily explains Ripple's distributed ledger technology, as a "consensus of shared and synchronised digital data." Bitcoin, for instance, does not function on a distributed ledger technology (DTL) since the network runs on a proof-of-work blockchain. This is an indication right away that the song is subtly targeting Ripple (XRP).

In one of the scenes, Lisa and Professor Frink sit on a stack of cardboard boxes which only a few of them have a logo that resembles Amazon. This is an interesting catch since Amazon and Ripple have a stealthy partnership, which ironically Ripple CEO Brad Garlinghouse has publicly claimed that Ripple aims to be the Amazon of the crypto sector. This again puts Ripple at the forefront of cryptocurrencies in which the episode could be trying to foreshadow the future developments.

Going back to Mr. Burns devious plan, the mathematicians claimed that they cannot create a better cryptocurrency but would rather come up with a formula to try and decrease the value of Frinkcoin. The only problem with the formula is that it would take them years to solve, so Mr. Burns puts a whiteboard with the below equation in the centre of the town in hopes that someone will pass by and solve the mysterious formula. At the end of the episode, only Lisa and the viewers are left knowing that Professor Frink was the one who self-destructively solved the equation of how to breach the security for his own cryptocurrency.

$\exists$ Bitcoin, Litecoin, Dogecoin, Frinkcoin $\Leftrightarrow$ SHA-256 is secure

Prove $\nexists$ secure SHA-256

$\exists$ secure $\Leftrightarrow$ RSA is correct

SHA-256 $\Leftrightarrow$ M^{ed} $\equiv$ M mod n $\forall$ M E $\mathbb{Z}$

               (n=pq, p8q prime, ed $\equiv$ 1 mod Φ (n))

               $\Leftrightarrow$ a ^{p-1} $\equiv$ 1   mod p $\forall$ aE $\mathbb{Z}$

               $\Leftrightarrow$ a & p $\neq$ 0   and a $\neq$ o mod p

               but   a&p = 0 Since 2015, when A&P went bankrupt!

$\therefore$ Bitcoin, Litecoin, Dogecoin, Frinkcoin   Q.E.D.

Knowing that the writers for the Simpsons are mathematical wizards, I asked a math whiz to explain the deeper meaning of the above equation that appeared in the episode. After all the math gibberish that seemed like a foreign language, the underlying message of the equation is trying to prove if the coins mentioned on the top row (Bitcoin, Litecoin, Dogecoin and Frinkcoin) is SHA-265 secure, which is currently one of the strongest cryptographic hash algorithms on the market. The bottom row concludes that the mentioned coins don't really exist in the sense of being RSA correct/SHA-265 secure.

Another strange comparison within the equation on the second last line makes the connection to the U.S. grocery store A&P, which went bankrupt in 2015. Could this freeze-gag equation be foreshadowing the destruction of most cryptocurrencies as SHA-265 isn't as secure as we are led to believe? Interestingly enough, XRP does not run-on SHA-265 and was not factored into the equation to prove that these cryptocurrencies will be worthless. Another strange coincidence was the article published on Yahoo Finance in 2019 titled, "Brad Garlinghouse says 99% of cryptocurrencies will probably go to zero." Maybe The Simpsons is trying to foreshadow that the trust in Bitcoin, Litecoin and Dogecoin will soon fade away.

In regard to Jim Parsons' guest appearance, many fans expressed their confusion online as to why he was the chosen one to explain what cryptocurrency is since he has no involvement within the sector. However, I couldn't help but make a connection to the European Central Bank due to its "Big Bang Migration" (ISO 20022) event scheduled for November 22nd, 2022. As previously discussed in chapter 2, this complex migration process is a pivotal day within the banking industry due to the European Central Bank, national central banks across Europe, all major market infrastructure providers and big financial firms, will simultaneously switch to the new ISO 20022 standards on the scheduled date.

To dig into the episode even further, there are many crypto fanatics online who have attempted to deconstruct hidden messages by using Gematria. The official Yale website explains Gematria as a Hebrew alphanumeric form of numerology that links a numerical value to coding names, words or phrases based on each specific letter. This is how messages are delivered on a mass scale hidden in plain sight.

Simple English Gematria Chart

A = 1	J = 10	S = 19
B = 2	K = 11	T = 20
C = 3	L = 12	U = 21
D = 4	M = 13	V = 22
E = 5	N = 14	W = 23
F = 6	O = 15	X = 24
G = 7	P = 16	Y = 25
H = 8	Q = 17	Z = 26
I = 9	R = 18	

By using the word "disco" as an example and calculating the value for each letter, it would equal the value of 50.

D - 4
I - 9
S - 19
C - 3
O - 15

Other words that also total 50 are owl, America and lion for instance. Many Gematria calculators online, such as gematrix.org, easily convert the calculations to showcase a list of equivalent words or phrases that contain the same numerical value to eliminate doing the calculations yourself.

This seemed absolutely bonkers at first, until I tested it out myself. The scene that drew me in the most within the whole episode were the scenes that took place in Moe's bar. I assumed that some of the wording on the bottles in the bar in the background would be a part of the writers freeze gag, so out of curiosity I typed many of the contorted wording into a Gematria calculator. To my surprise, all the searches had a peculiar theme that shockingly aligned with another. The ones that popped out the most were on the Absolut bottle that stated "absolu kru" which in Gematria translates to "December Seven" and instead of Moet, the bottle read "Moe et Chandon," which equals to "Market Crash" in Gematria.

The odd coincidence within the episode had multiple translations resorting back to the date of December 7th as a frantic warning of a sell off since it looked as if there was an expected market crash on the horizon. To stir the pot even more, in past Simpsons' episodes, clocks have been notorious for secretly portraying important dates backwards. In this episode, Homer wrote a note to Marge that he will be late and the time on the clock was set to 12:08 with "home late - H", which I thought had a deeper meaning.

By using the ridiculous concept of Gematria, I took a massive risk and sold my XRP position on December 7th, 2020 strictly due to analysing the hidden messages within the Frinkcoin episode. A few days passed and XRP investors were celebrating the fact that XRP doubled in price from November to December and were expecting the price to skyrocket even more. Meanwhile, I was silently keeping to myself because I foolishly sold my position because of an absurd Simpsons conspiracy. I started to doubt myself and reality started to settle in that I made the biggest trading mistake of my life that was based on complete nonsense.

It wasn't until waking up on December 22nd, 2020 when Brad Garlinghouse announced on Twitter that the SEC was filing a lawsuit against Ripple. My jaw dropped to the floor and I had to pinch myself because the price of XRP plummeted from £0.41 down to £0.12 a few days later and investors were publicly expressing their anger online. I bought back my XRP position while there was blood on the street and have the Simpsons to thank for the most profound trade I have ever made to date. Was this a coincidence or pure luck?

To fall down the rabbit hole of conspiracy theories even more, the word "frink" in Gematria is the equivalent to "XRP" and "Frinkcoin" which coincidently, has the same Gematria value as the name of 'BearableGuy'. The significance of @Bearableguy123 is that the account is a mysterious Twitter and Reddit 'riddler' within the XRP cryptosphere which may believe is a Ripple insider. The account @Bearableguy123, @Yuglebaraeb123 and @looP_rM311_7211 are all believed to be the same insider since their posts showcase a lot of foreshadowing images and cryptic riddles of the future developments of Ripple that *some* investors enjoy deconstructing. Many believe that Bearable Guy is Brad Garlinghouse or David Schwartz, the Chief Technology Officer for Ripple, but that will forever remain as one of life's tucked away secrets.

To stir the pot even more, Schwartz used to be a Cryptographer Consultant for The National Security Agency (NSA), which has led some tin foil hat investors to assume that Schwartz was privately hired to join a team to create

Bitcoin under the pseudonym Satoshi Nakamoto. Before Bitcoin became the pioneer coin in 2009, David Schwartz also interestingly filed a patent (number 5,025,369) for a similar network to Bitcoin in 1988. This is ironically the same year the Economist magazine published its notorious cover that stated, "get ready for a world currency." A fun theory to also dwell on is the belief that Bitcoin is a live test before the chosen digital reserve currency (XRP or XLM) will be mass adopted. By humoring this theory in conjunction with the plot of the Simpsons' episode, the writers could be foreshadowing the fall of Bitcoin. In the episode, the original creator of the coin became the self-destructive reason for its downfall, which makes me question if Bitcoin was to ever fail due to the original creators (my guess is Ripple's c-level management team) sabotaging the networks' trust. If this happens, XRP or XLM could very well rise out of the ashes as the phoenix to be the global digital reserve currency. Interestingly enough, Bitcoin and Ripple were also coincidentally issued using the same IP address (64.202.167.192) so the plot keeps thickening on the head-scratching coincidences between the two cryptos.

In a freeze frame gag that quickly sneakily popped on the screen for 5 seconds was a large paragraph of gibberish that did not make any sense. However, the last paragraph stated, "we know who Satoshi is but we're not telling." What a wonderful way to dangle a carrot in front of crypto fanatics. It wouldn't surprise me that the creators know who Satoshi is, but it would be hilarious if David Schwartz was Satoshi Nakamoto or that he is part of the 'future plans' to destroy the trust of the Bitcoin system as the episode showcased. Although Schwartz has publicly denied the rumours that he is Satoshi Nakamoto, isn't that what someone would say if they're trying to keep their identity secret? Clark Kent wouldn't admit that he's Superman, so why would Satoshi reveal their real identity?

Although the above conspiracies are to be taken lightly, part of the XRP community has been a laughingstock from 'serious' investors for many years now. Conspiracies like this have created a divide online of those who believe the tin foil hat conspiracy theories and those who find it as utter rubbish. Although this is all fun and games, it's hard to deny the reputation The Simpsons has of predictive programming. Before my tin foil hat gets too tight, what are your thoughts on the manner? Has The Simpsons added another iconic prediction to add to the ever-growing list or was this episode just silly banter to stay relevant to the ongoing trends in today's society? Only time will tell.

Kendra Hill

The second conspiracy theory is an extremely speculative, yet interesting string of predictions to absorb since the information was presented on a blog by an anonymous 'whistle-blower' with the pseudonym of Kendra Hill. The frustrating part is that the initial blog posts on Steemit were deleted after it received a lot of attention. Maybe she was threatened after exposing the truth or it was all a lie and she couldn't handle any negative backlash. We'll never know the truth until the next few years, however, what we do have is the blog archive from @Dewar_Phil as proof of the initial posts. Although a lot of information about her has been buried online, if you search Kendra Hill XRP and look at the images section on Google, a lot of screenshots of her old posts appear for clarity.

Introducing herself to the public in July 2018, she stated that she has been an investor within the crypto sector since 2016 and has insider information due to having a family of prominent investment bankers. A lot of people were quick to dismiss Hill, yet many grew fond of her blog posts since she confidently had a few predictions come true and welcomed any questions since the purpose of her blog was to, "help people reach a high level of success, so they can live the life that they desire."

She made some shocking statements and hooked readers' attention by stating that Ripple is fabricating its main focus on managing cross-border payments, as their end goal is to tackle the quadrillion dollar derivatives market. She also predicted that one of Ripple's biggest international partners was going to enter the derivatives market and then 25 days later, she created a post to prove that she was right. Unfortunately, some of the links she posted on her blog have mysteriously vanished off the other news outlets, but if you Google "SBI Holdings enters derivatives market," a few articles will appear if you want to dig deeper.

Explaining her reasoning for how Ripple will manage the *entire* quadrillion dollar derivatives market is by partnering with Codius, since they bring smart contracts to the table. While researching the advancements of Codius, Coindesk reported that Ripple parted ways, yet Kendra Hill noted that it was a lie and Codius is very much still involved in the plans. As discussed in chapter 3, a similar partnership with Flare has made some investors believe that Flare is Codius 2.0. Flare brings everything Codius could have brought to the table with smart contracts, but apparently more. The best way to describe the difference is if you compare Codius and Flare together as calculators. Codius would have shown you the answers, whereas Flare would have provided the answers along with the proof. Although there is not a lot of recent news about Codius, if Kendra is correct by saying that Codius is still in the picture, the combination of Flare, Codius and Ripple is a force to be reckoned with when it comes to tackling the derivatives market. This is due to the deadly combination of smart contracts, integrated with fast and inexpensive payment processes along with a variety of privacy options.

As if she couldn't get any more bullish on XRP, she boldly stated that investors only need 2000 XRP to become a part of the 1% since she claims that XRP will be worth more than one gold ounce around 2027, which is roughly $1864 each. Now let's do some math and entertain her idea for fun. The current price of XRP is $0.28, so if you were to buy 2000 XRP, you'd only need to spend $560 (2000*0.28). If you'd hold onto your position for dear life within the next decade, using Kendra's prediction (1864*2000), you could have a groundbreaking $3,728,000! I'll give you time to let that sink in and have a chuckle to yourself because that would be hilarious if XRP actually hits 4 digits. Imagine having a couple of hundreds laying around to invest and you bought 2000 XRP as a joke because of a conspiracy and you forgot about it overtime, only to realise a few years later that you're a millionaire by 2027!? Comical gold right there. It seems too good to be true, however, David Schwartz tweeted on November 21st, 2017 to discuss why XRP can't function properly for financial institutions at a cheap price.

> "It *can't* be dirt cheap. That doesn't make any sense. If XRP costs $1, they'd need a million XRP which would cost $1 million. If XRP costs a million dollars, they'd need one XRP which would, again, cost $1 million. Except that higher prices make payments cheaper. Right now, you can buy a million-dollar house with Bitcoin. When Bitcoin was $300, it would move the market too much and be too expensive to be practical. So higher prices make payments cheaper."

It is outrageous for some investors to believe that a 4 digit XRP is attainable, however, not many people thought 1 Bitcoin would hit $10 in the earlier days, let alone $40,000 in January 2021. As a result, anything is quite literally possible within this volatile, yet speculative market.

> "5 years from now it will be the upper-class that is in possession of almost the entire supply of XRP. It is not meant for the lower-class. However, at this moment in time someone from the lower-class can buy/hold XRP allowing them to move up in the world. I call it the token of freedom."

Back in 2018, Kendra Hill predicted that the rate at which the crypto market hits a "trillion-dollar market cap will be shockingly fast," which just happened in January 2021. Hill mentioned that there were delays in future plans and mentioned that the New York Stock Exchange is going to release a crypto exchange called Bakkt. Funnily enough, on January 12, 2021, Bitcoin.com released an article titled, "Crypto Futures Exchange Bakkt Going Public at a Valuation of $2.1 Billion." If we assume that what she was saying had a 2-year delay, then her future predictions perfectly lines us up for 2021 as we have just entered a bull market, which she states will be "a bull market unlike any that has been seen before." She also warns that an economic collapse is looming on the horizon and banks are stress testing emergency services to prevent chaos. To stir the pot even more, her posts took a dark turn by stating that the first half of the new decade will decide the fate of humanity and will be an uphill battle. Coronavirus has entered the chat - an uphill battle indeed.

To entertain the idea of a global currency, Hill stated that cryptocurrency will be made illegal in many years to come. She warned that:

> *"...allowing additional currencies to exist when the world is only using one would be disruptive so it will not be tolerated and it will be easier to stop than you think. The illusion is that Bitcoin (for example) is untouchable - the reality is that it is government controlled through the use of mining pools."*

It is interesting that she said that because Brad Garlinghouse has publicly stated on Anthony Pompliano's podcast in 2020 that China controls over 50% of the Bitcoin mining pools. Hill continues to say that, "any cryptocurrency aiming to be a decentralised digital currency will not survive" and she emphasised that the one global currency has already been chosen. That coin is Stellar Lumen (XLM). Hill compared XLM and XRP as 'brother and sister' and deemed XLM as digital silver and XRP as digital gold. She claims that XRP was never meant to be a currency, but rather a store of value and that "Ripple and Stellar are the keys to the new world financial system." To try and make sense of such a bold statement, Dewar Phil mentioned that having XLM as the world's digital currency is not a far-fetched plan since Stellar is a non-profit. He also suggested that the organisation can donate money to the "World Bank (or some other global governance body)."

Before the IMF and various governments within Canada, the US and UK, for example, were publicly discussing a "global reset", Hill claimed back in 2018 that a global reset is in motion and that we should have a new world government by 2025. This is incredibly hard to imagine, especially when certain countries can't even agree on how to handle a viral outbreak during the 2020 pandemic. Thus, how can all nations come together to agree on a one world government? Let's humour this idea though - could the destruction that the world faces early in the new decade be the glue that ultimately unites nations together to create a happy Kumbaya moment in history?

To think of the New World Order conspiracies coming into fruition can be laughable to dwell on, but when Ripple CEO Brad Garlinghouse was a key speaker at the Paris FinTech Forum in 2019, he stated that "we are moving in a New World Order." It's funny when random people online joke about a "New World Order" but when key figures within the industry start talking about it as well, it's a bit of a head-scratching moment.

To connect the dots even more and to tie in another *odd* conspiracy theory, is to discuss the queen of vogue's 2019 Eurovision performance. If you're interested, do a quick search for Madonna's performance on YouTube and keep your eyes peeled for the eerie occult symbolism throughout. The comments section of the video alone is quite comical to read, having fans call her performance a "ritual", but what jumped out at me right away was the XRP and Stellar Lumen logo on her robe and eye patch. Coincidentally, David Schwartz used to have a cartoon photo of him wearing the same eye patch as his Twitter photo.

At the time of the performance, Corona was still a beloved beer and an infectious virus was not of anyone's concern, but the visual element of the performance had some frightening similarities to how disastrous the year 2020 turned out to be. The lyrics that Madonna sang also complimented the destruction shown on the screens by singing, *"not everyone is coming to the future."* It was quite ironic to hear considering that a year later, life was put on hold and the world was hit with the Coronavirus outbreak. Towards the end of the performance, two dancers bring the Palestinian and Israeli flag together by linking arms to create an infinity symbol (potentially hinting at a one world government), which many fans were outraged by the controversy. The performance ended with Madonna whispering "Wake Up" while the phrase was boldly stated on the LED screen.

To tie in Kendra's blog posts to the performance, there are a few similarities that overlap – the destruction of the beginning of the new decade, along with the introduction of a one world government and a new world reserve currency. Take what you want from this performance, but it's hard to deny the eerie similarities linked that are questionable.

Before Kendra mysteriously deleted all her blog posts, she stated, "People may not believe what I say today, and I do not expect anyone to. When the time comes and the truths are revealed, you will realise that I am someone you should listen to." To this day, the identity of Kendra is still a mystery to the XRP community. However, just when fans thought she vanished forever, she updated her blog in 2021 to link her new Twitter account - @cryptokendra.

Although her Twitter has only been active for 4 days when writing this, she claimed that she will use her account to help followers build wealth due to having access to classified information. Some of the information she releases can be a bit out of the ordinary for some to grasp, however, her aim is to tear down the walls of the illusion within the reality we live in - regardless if you believe her or not. With all her bold claims, Kendra has a mix of reviews from firm believers and those who think she's bluffing. One of her tweets stated, "Imagine having all the answers to a test and then having someone tell you that you're going to fail it. Is their opinion going to affect you? Lol."

To gain credibility, she started leaving breadcrumbs to those who want to fall down the rabbit hole, but due to the early inception of her account, she said to be patient and time will tell if all her 'predictions' become reality. In the meantime, I have my popcorn ready and signed up to her Twitter alerts to keep track of her future announcements. Regardless if she's right or not, I find her posts juicier than a gossip magazine, so sign me up for a life time membership.

The Economist 1988 Cover

The third conspiracy theory is in regard to the infamous 1988 cover of the Economist magazine. A quick backstory of the Economist is that the Rothschild's (one of the most powerful banking families in the world) are amongst the few 'A' special shareholders and are actually part owners, which is stated on The Economist Group official website. Due to a lot of powerful financial figures having ties to the magazine, there are several online communities that find joy in decoding the covers in which people believe that there are hidden messages that foreshadow the outcome of the future economy in plain sight.

For copyright reasons, I can't show the cover within the book, however, if you Google "1988 Economist magazine," you can see the controversial cover for yourself. I recommend searching for the cover before reading ahead to try and see if you can pick up on any symbolism yourself. However, if you don't have access to the internet at the moment, the initial headline on the cover sets the theme by stating, "Get ready for a world currency," with the focal point as a large phoenix on top of a pile of global fiat money that is burning. Right off the bat, this reflects back to the ancient Greek folklore tale where a phoenix rises from the ashes after a catastrophic event to be more powerful and stronger than before. On the neck of the Phoenix is a gold chain with a gold coin attached that states on the perimeter, "Ten Phoenix 2018." The number 10 is also boldly visible and in the centre of the coin there is a circle with a diagonal line that resembles the planet Saturn.

To discuss a contrarian view of a global currency, Martin Armstrong, who is an "Agenda Contributor" for the World Economic Forum and funnily enough a convicted felon for securities fraud, voiced a negative outlook of the cover on his official website back in 2017. Armstrong explained that if a global currency was to become the norm, a single government would emerge by 'force' and political change would require a 'bloodbath in revolution.' As someone who has a history of being the Strategic Crisis Manager for many major financial crisis events such as the 1987 Stock Market Crash and the 1997 Asian Financial Currency Crisis, it is compelling to read that he strongly feels that a 'monumental collapse' would be the only logical route to a global currency. Hmmm...now what can possibly trigger the economic downfall of the entire world? Ah yes, that's right...good ol' COVID-19 has now entered the chat. As catastrophic as the pandemic has been, even Lord Rothschild described the pandemic as "a distraction" in a 2020 interview with his daughter Hannah Rothschild when discussing the technological solutions for the future of the economy.

The U.S. financial reaction to COVID-19 has resulted in a weaker U.S. dollar and to add to the existing chaos of the economic downturn, a stock market crash and a black swan event is also looming right around the corner in 2021 or 2022. With a stack of economic crises piling up to start the new decade off, a global currency is positioned perfectly more than ever to rise out of the ashes as the Economist magazine suggested.

When taking a deep dive into the article of what to expect for a global currency, the author stated that, "prices will be quoted not in dollars, yen or D-marks but in, let's say, the phoenix. The phoenix will be favoured by companies and shoppers because it will be more convenient than today's national currencies." The article also highlighted the positive usage of a global currency that would accelerate *opportunities* for international trade and investment contracts:

"This too is the gift of advancing technology. Falling transport costs will make it easier for countries thousands of miles apart to compete in each other's markets. The law of one price (that a good should cost the

same everywhere, once prices are converted into a single currency) will increasingly assert itself. Politicians permitting that national economies will follow their financial markets - becoming ever more open to the outside world. This will apply to labour as much as to goods, partly through migration but also through technology's ability to separate the worker from the point at which he delivers his labour. Indian computer operators will be processing New Yorkers' pay checks."

To gear back to analysing the Economist cover, I noticed that on top of the Phoenix's head was the fleur-de-lys emblem. This caught my attention since the emblem has a deep religious and political meaning in history that represents noble power, rebirth, unity and most relatable in this situation – light. When breaking down the name Stellar Lumen, stellar literally means to shine "like a star" and lumen, is the standard unit of luminous flux which is the human eyes' perception of a force of light. The contextual significance as a whole exudes a new beginning since light on a universal level symbolises the illuminated source of divine goodness, unity and regeneration.

When trying to dig deep into the significance of the gold coin hanging from the phoenix's neck, I realised that in Latin, X is the equivalent number to 10. When looking at the list of the top 100 cryptocurrencies, only XLM and XRP started with the letter X. Coincidentally, the circle with the line struck through was the exact Stellar Lumen logo before it was changed to what it is today, which still looks quite similar. This could potentially foreshadow that Stellar Lumen is the chosen 'phoenix coin' that was mentioned in the article to bring the global economy out of the ashes that it is currently in. Although the year 2018 on the coin can be misleading since it is currently 2021 and we have yet to have a global currency per se, the final sentence of the article stated, "pencil in the phoenix for *around* 2018, and welcome it when it comes." Emphasis on *around* 2018, which indicates that this shift can still be looming around the corner since Kendra Hill also stated that plans have been "delayed."

Final Conspiracy Thoughts

In a world full of chaos, conspiracies like this can tickle the curious of minds to think outside the box. Maybe it's all true and buying into the hype will get you rich, or it's complete bullshit and you'll save your money rather than feed into the nonsense. Believe it or don't believe it, either way, the conspiracies presented are amusing merely for entertainment purposes. Only time will tell the outcome that will unfold before 2030, but one thing for certain is that I'll have my popcorn ready and a front row ticket to the unravelling of how the crypto sector will pan out.

13

What Does the Future Have in Store?

"Whenever you make an investment in yourself,
you're making an investment in your future."

- Anonymous

As I look into my imaginative crystal ball, the advancements of the cryptocurrency sector will continue to revamp the future of finance, business and economics on a global scale. We have come a long way from lugging around gold bars to use as a means of exchange for goods and services, to now being able to simplify transactions with the evolution of decentralised innovation. With inflation rates continuing to rise after detaching from a gold standard, the downfall of the COVID-19 crisis has thrown the global economy into a frenzy where trillions of dollars are being printed out of thin air to cope with the negative backlash of the pandemic. As a result, it is only a matter of time before the constant money printing will backfire since the economy is acting like a kettle that's about to blow.

The *trusted* media paints a picture that life a year after the global pandemic is gearing back to normality. However, the reality is that the economy may never fully recover to get back to what life used to be like before the coronavirus. To give a warning of what the future may hold, Harvard economist and financial crises expert Kenneth S. Rogoff stated that he, "feels like the 2008 financial crisis was just a dry run." If that's not alarming enough, he goes on to say that the global pandemic "is already shaping up as the deepest dive on record for the global economy for over 100 years. Everything depends on how long it lasts, but if this goes on for a long time, it's certainly going to be the mother of all financial crises." Thanks pal for those encouraging words.

In an aid to help the American economy though, the U.S. government has made it evident that until the GDP and job rates are back up after the COVID-19 crisis, they won't steer away from the unparalleled money printing. However, regardless of the COVID-19 crisis, the economy was bound for a stock market crash in 2021 or 2022. With this in conjunction with stimulus cheques continuing to be handed out like Halloween candy, the devaluation of the American dollar will progressively push retail and institutional investors towards the cryptocurrency market as a hedge against inflation.

Professor Klaus Schwab who is the Founder and Executive Chairman of the World Economic Forum, has even stated that life after the coronavirus pandemic will never get back to "normal." He stated that "the pandemic represents a rare but narrow window of opportunity to reflect, reimagine, and reset our world." The irony with a global reset is that conspiracy theorists were openly discussing the concept between 2017-2019 but were getting slated to give attention to such a foolish theory. With the bombshell of COVID-19 spreading worldwide, the conspiracy theory turned into a reality with global figures such as Justin Trudeau, Boris Johnston and even the Prince of Wales publicly promoted "the great reset" as part of the radical Coronavirus Recovery Campaign to "build back better" the global economy. There have been mixed opinions on a global reset, but the harsh reality is that the reset is in motion regardless of the general public's personal vendetta against the concept. If you don't want to be affected by the reset, then move to a segregated community where you can truly escape the shackles from the powers that be. Otherwise, there is not much we can do other than anticipate, accept and strategically profit off of the reset with its ties to the cryptocurrency sector.

With the World Economic Forum spearheading the 'resetting of the digital currencies' game plan, I expect a huge financial shift of wealth to occur from 2020-2027 where the digitisation of global currencies will become the new norm. Through this transition into a new digital benchmark, I believe by 2030 physical cash will be a distant memory due to the mass adoption of Central Bank Digital Currencies (CBDCs). As a result, certain cryptocurrencies and blockchain technologies will be ingrained into our society without the general public even realising. Respectively, the same nonchalant stance on how our computers function will be the same mindset in the powering force behind CBDCs – casually utilising it without thinking of the motherboard functionalities. The extraordinary aspect in this global shift of wealth is that only a small percentage of the world's population is aware of this rare goldmine opportunity and if you're reading this book, then you're one of the lucky few. Cha-ching!

With the rise of CBDCs on a global scale, countries such as China, Sweden, Bahamas, France, Jamaica and Ukraine, for instance, are paving the path to digitise their fiat ahead of other countries. In a survey issued in early 2021, the Bank for International Settlements (BIS) confirmed that 86% of central banks on an international scale are attentively analysing the powerful effects of CBDCs. Whether we like it or not, the COVID-19 pandemic has catapulted the adoption of a cashless society and the cryptos working alongside governments and banks will help with the transition. Starbucks, Tesco and Whole Foods, for instance, are amongst the list of stores that have posted a sign upon checkout to refuse physical fiat as a preventative to not transmit germs. Sounds like a perfect transition into a cashless society don't you think?

Many people in the west are outraged because physical money is legal tender and are sharing in-depth lists on social media which claim that leaving money for the tooth fairy, giving money to the homeless, going to a car boot (garage) sales, doing odd jobs and leaving money in birthday cards for instance, will be completely swept away. This is false. Although the physical aspect of bills and coins will be removed from these acts, the ability to transfer money in these situations still remains valid. A perfect glimpse into how a cashless society functions is to analyse the financial technological advancements happening in China and Sweden.

The act of transferring money in China simply relies on a scannable QR code on a piece of laminated paper or plastic a4 stand for shops. Powered by the two dominating mobile payment apps Alipay and WeChat, citizens can casually scan barcodes upon checkout or in advance to verify the amount on the app for the money to be transferred in a matter of seconds. Instead of a bill in a card, there will be a paper with a QR code to scan. See a performance on the street by a busker and want to tip? Scan their barcode. See a homeless individual on the street? Scan their code. Want to buy fresh vegetables at a market? Scan the stalls' QR code.

In a totalitarian country such as China where privacy is abused, citizens were skeptical at first to transition into a cashless society, but after WeChat and Alipay were integrated into their everyday life, many citizens preferred this futuristic method of payment since it's more convenient. An interesting survey for how citizens in China regard their cashless society, was carried out by Ipsos, which is the world's third-largest market research company. The study showcased that any doubts about a cashless society at first fizzled away as the FinTech integration became the norm. The convenience, speed, decrease of theft and accessibility debate outweighed the negative and pushed cash to become a distant memory – with a mild and understandable exception with the elderly. Below are the highlighted stats from the study:

- *40% of people regularly carry less than £11.40 in cash*

- *74% of people said they can live with only £11.40 in cash for more than a month*

- *84% of people feel calm if they don't carry cash, 12% concerned and 4% refusal*

- *7 out of 10 people in China make use of a virtual wallet. This compares to 5/10 in the U.S*

With WeChat in China being the equivalent social blend to what Facebook, Instagram and YouTube are, the adoption of a mobile payment exchange ingrained into the app was a clever ploy to target millions of existing users. The same concept has now been hijacked by Facebook with the platforms' plan to create its own cryptocurrency, titled the Libra at first but then changed to Diem. Although the Diem is in no position to overtake the U.S. dollar, Diem at first provided a hurdle for the U.S. to produce a globally accepted digital currency, which was the nail in the coffin for central banks to finally take digital currencies seriously. Instead of offering a basket of cryptocurrencies as initially planned, Facebook now plans to launch Diem in 2021 as its own stablecoin that will be pegged to the US dollar. Introducing Diem to the platform's millions of users could spark interest in other digital currencies and could be a driving force of distancing millions away from physical money out of ease of use. Nonetheless, it will be interesting to see how Diem will or won't be accepted by Facebook users – especially since Facebook has a scandalous past of breaching user's data.

In the continuance of a cashless society, Sweden will be the first country in the entire world to go completely cashless in March of 2023, while China has already accelerated the race to a central bank-backed digitised fiat – DCEP, acronym for digital currency electronic payment. The ironic humour of a cashless society in China is that the country invented paper money in the 9th century and is now trying to get rid of it all together. Good old irony.

Although Sweden will be the first country to go completely cashless, China's digitalisation of its currency is currently battling the forefront of being the next world reserve currency, which is in its final testing phase as of 2021. This poses a huge threat to the U.S. as a globally accepted digital currency can very much reduce the ruling influence of the American dollar on global trade. Although America is *publicly* trailing behind the race to a digitalised fiat, there are definitely plans brewing behind closed doors to hint otherwise.

In an effort to gear back to the gold standard, President Trump's nominee for the Federal Reserve's Board of Governors, Judy Shelton, is a public figure advocating the use of cryptocurrency as a modernised gold standard. At her Senate confirmation hearing in February 2020, she stated that the U.S. desperately needs FinTech modifications to stay ahead of other countries and suggested that digitising the U.S. dollar could help maintain the currency's dominance in global commerce. Shelton claimed that, "rival nations are working very diligently to have an alternative to the dollar, and I think it is very important that we get ahead of the curve to ensure that the dollar continues to offer the best currency in the world [...] in a very cryptocurrency way."

Joining Shelton as a positive advocate for a global digital currency is the former Bank of England governor, Mark Carney. As a previous skeptic to now being a firm believer in cryptocurrency, Carney espoused his belief that a global digital currency similar to Bitcoin could take the leading spot of the world's reserve currency beating the U.S. dollar. According to Yahoo Finance, Carney has publicly stated that "the relatively high costs of domestic and cross border electronic payments are encouraging innovation, with new entrants applying new technologies to offer lower cost and more convenient retail payment services." Sound familiar? Seems awfully similar to XRP and XLM's use case.

To also chime in on the matter, the World Economic Forum also agreed with an article posted on their main website titled, "A Digital Currency Should Be Adopted As The World's Leading Reserve Currency." Although going back to the old gold standard is not an option, a new modernised twist to the Bretton Woods Agreement could be brewing in the future. This can be done by going back to a gold-backed currency by using the fundamentals of what makes cryptocurrencies so cutting-edge.

In addition to Judy Shelton and Mark Carney, European Central Bank president Christine Lagarde, is one of the key figures to keep an eye on when it comes to paving the path to a new and more modernised monetary system. In an interview with CNBC, she told Elizabeth Schulze, "I think anything that is using distributed ledger technology, whether you call it crypto, assets, currencies or whatever [...] is clearly shaking the system and it's far from the Bitcoin that we used to talk about a year ago." To expand on her views, Lagarde wrote an article in November 2020 titled, "The Future Of Money – Innovating While Retaining Trust," where she stated that the overall amount of non-cash payments continues to increase across Europe. This increased by 8.1 percent to 98 billion over the past year and almost half of these transactions were carried out by card, followed by direct debits and credit transfers.

As Bitcoin becomes more popular, the instinctive negative assumption will continue to cloud skeptic's minds and as expected, financial institutions will initially speak ill of Bitcoin since it poses a large threat against the current monetary system. The amusing occurrence came when chairman and CEO of JP Morgan, Jamie Dimon, slammed Bitcoin in 2017 for publicly announcing that he would fire any JP Morgan employee who discussed Bitcoin. He even slandered his daughter publicly for buying into the hype. By being so vocal about his bitterness over the digital currency, it came as a shock when the firm's quantitative experts announced in October 2020 that Bitcoin is likely to 10 X the value of gold and is an appropriate alternative to gold. Interesting change of opinion since the fundamentals never changed but better late than never, right?

To continue with the bullish news, an insightful Cointelegraph YouTube video titled, "Institutional Money to Propel Bitcoin to Over $250K in One Year?", interviewed CEO and founder of Real Vision and Global Macro Investor Raoul Pal, to explain his thoughts on why 2021 will be an explosive year for Bitcoin. He confidently stated that the 2017 bull run for the last Bitcoin halving event were only retail buyers, which contrastingly predicted that the bull run of 2021 will be more powerful due to the large institutional (smart money) interest on top of retail investors. As a result, there will be an astounding amount of money introduced to the market that could propel the price to reach all-time highs since "the real money is interested and that's a game changer." Pal goes on to state that since PayPal, Square, and Greyscale have started accumulating Bitcoin (PayPal alone at a staggering 70%), this has now created a scarcity issue that many are fearful of, which leaves a shortage of coins. To finish the interview, he pointed out that the macroeconomic factors are playing in Bitcoin's favour and bullishly stated, "I've never seen a market with this supply and demand imbalance before."

To finish 2020 on a high note, a Citibank investors report leaked to the public that exposed its target of Bitcoin hitting $318,000 by the end of 2021, which also deemed Bitcoin as the digital gold of the modern era. The foundation of the report was based on the decline of the U.S. dollar as the world's reserve currency and the report pointed out that the first Bitcoin bull cycle from 2011 to 2013, emerged from the last recession as it increased by 555 times. The report also noted that gold is likely to gain from the economic downfall as well but has constraints such as storage, non-portability and could even be deemed "yesterday's news" in terms of a financial hedge. By deeming Bitcoin better than gold, Citibank MD backed its statement by highlighting the scarcity of Bitcoin by only having a limited supply (21 million) and the fact that it is easier to transfer across borders.

While it is great to finally see well-known banks, public figures and companies such as PayPal join the crypto sector to get a slice of the pie, Ripple getting sued by the SEC acts as a potential warning that more lawsuits could blossom as we enter a new quantum financial system within the next decade. In an interview with Bloomberg, Ripple CEO Brad Garlinghouse boldly stated that he believes that 99% of cryptocurrencies will vanish and "go to zero." He also stated that he believes that we're "going to continue to see consolidation. The world doesn't need 3000+ cryptocurrencies out there and I think the utility will bear out that there will be a migration to quality if you will." As harsh as it may seem, I have to agree with his prediction as I strongly feel that the 1% of cryptocurrencies that thrive will be the ones solving real world issues and are not rebelling against the powers that be.

Bitcoin introduced the world to blockchain technology, which is now being utilised for measures far beyond the world of finance, which is fantastic, but due to Bitcoin's decentralised manner, the factor of *trust* is the pivotal reason for its success since no authority can meddle. As a result, governments and central banks around the world have expressed an equal hatred for the pioneer cryptocurrency since they don't have control over it. In this predicament, what can governments do to try and take down Bitcoin if they can't control it? They can try to flip the narrative to get the public to turn against Bitcoin, so people don't have any trust in it anymore. If the trust starts to fade, then that's when the foundation can start to collapse just like the blocks in the game Jenga. The initial tower of blocks is a strong foundation, however, when you start to take out the pieces, in this case the element of trust, then the once sturdy structure will collapse.

As the crypto sector continues to soar, the mainstream media will continue to create fear, uncertainty and doubt (FUD) by claiming Bitcoin is "fake internet money," while also trying to spin a negative narrative that Bitcoin is predominantly used by criminals for money laundering. From afar it's understandable why people may assume that a digital currency that is anonymous could be used by criminals, however, the truth of the matter is that only 0.34% of cryptocurrency transactions have been accounted for illicit activities. This was down 2% from 2019 as reported by the blockchain firm, Chainalysis.

During the World Economic Forum's Davos agenda in 2021, Silver Lake Co-Founder Glenn Hutchins even admitted that since physical fiat is "untraceable and fungible," 90% of $100 American dollar bills are "used for organised crime and tax evasion." Messari also reported that fiat currencies are 800 times more commonly used on the black market than cryptocurrencies, so it's quite hard to deny the facts rather than being spoon fed with lies against a currency that poses a threat to the future of the monetary system. Although these news stories are all smoke and mirrors, there are four major threats to Bitcoin that should be taken seriously – higher taxes, a '6102 attack', the fact that 65% of Bitcoins mining pools are located in China and Tether's infamous lawsuit.

To deter the trust away from Bitcoin's groundbreaking and innovative technology, I do fear that governments on a global scale could impose higher taxes where anyone holding Bitcoin could get taxed an arm and a leg. This would throw people off from wanting to touch it. In addition, U.S. President Franklin D. Roosevelt signed Executive Order 6102 in 1933 to forbid the possession of gold bullion, gold certificates and gold coins, which even threatened offenders with jail time. There have not been any warning signs that this may happen, but it is concerning if history could be repeated as a

159

way for the governments to win against the fight against Bitcoin since it's considered digital gold.

Only time will tell but keeping a close eye on what those in power are publicly saying is key when determining what the future holds. By listening to Christine Lagarde talk, we can gage the potential direction of Bitcoin's future due to her negative stance by encouraging global regulations to be put in place. To join Lagarde with her bitter outlook on Bitcoin is Kenneth Rogoff, a Harvard professor of economics and former Chief Economist at the International Monetary Fund (IMF). He claimed that "governments will not allow Bitcoin to grow in popularity" and is confident that the government will prevail in the fight against the future of Bitcoin.

The third threat to Bitcoin was brought up by Ripple CEO Brad Garlinghouse who argued on Anthony Pompliano's podcast that 65% of Bitcoins mining pools that powers the blockchain are located in China. As a result of this bombshell, the geographical centralisation of having such a high-power source can pose concerns. This can be a problem if the Chinese Communist Party tries to intervene by cutting the power supply to the miners due to the conflicting stance of cryptocurrencies within the country.

The last but certainly not least threat that is looming in the distance for Bitcoin is Tether's lawsuit, in which Ethereum's founder Buterin has stated on The Tim Ferriss Show in March 2021 that "Tether is Bitcoin's ticketing time bomb demon."

Before diving into the many flaws with Tether, a quick run-down of Tether (USDT) is that it is a 'stablecoin' that is supposed to be pegged to the American dollar 1:1, which aims to keep a stable amount of $1 to avoid the volatility of the crypto market. For a lot of exchanges other than Coinbase, converting fiat money to a stablecoin is needed before investing in cryptos, whereas on Coinbase, you can buy Bitcoin directly with fiat money without converting it to a stablecoin first. As a result of other exchanges relying on Tether as a clutch for trading, data by NYDIG reported that 50%-60% of Bitcoin trades for Tether.

Unlike other cryptocurrencies where there is a capped supply, Tether does not have a limited supply, so many critics, such as the University of Texas finance professor John Griffin, have noticed that there is a correlation that when millions or billions of USDT were 'printed,' the price of Bitcoin goes up and when Tether is not 'printed,' Bitcoin's price drops. By analysing millions of transactions with one of his graduate students, Amin Shams, their in-depth analysis was presented in a 66-page paper titled, "Is Bitcoin Really Un-Tethered?" in which they concluded that Tether was actually used to "stabilise and manipulate" Bitcoin on the exchange Bitfinex. To also chime in on the matter, a report issued by JP Morgan titled, "Perspectives - Digital Transformation and the Rise of FinTech: Blockchain, Bitcoin and Digital Finance 2021", boldly admitted that "a sudden loss of confidence in USDT would likely generate a severe liquidity shock, jeopardizing access to the largest pools of demand and liquidity." While there are investors who feel that the threat of Tether's downfall has been brushed under the carpet due to the lawsuit coming to a settlement in early 2021, there are also a handful of other investors that feel that this isn't the end of Tether's "ticking time bomb", as Buterin has robustly stated.

In a bid to put the public's mind at ease regarding Tether's lawsuit, the stablecoin's Twitter account tweeted, "Tether & @Bitfinex have reached a settlement with @NewYorkStateAG. After 2.5 years and 2.5M pages of info shared, we admit to no wrongdoing and will pay US$18.5M to resolve this matter." By reading this tweet at face value paints a reassuring picture that Tether's case is just dandy with a dash of rainbows and butterflies in lalaland since they, "admit to no wrongdoing." Contrastingly, a press release that was issued by the New York Attorney General's office on the same day had a different story to tell:

"Bitfinex and Tether recklessly and unlawfully covered-up massive financial losses to keep their scheme going and protect their bottom lines," said Attorney General James. "Tether's claims that its virtual currency was fully backed by U.S. dollars at all times was a lie. These companies obscured the true risk investors faced and were operated by unlicensed and unregulated individuals and entities dealing in the darkest corners of the financial system. This week, we're taking action to end Bitfinex and Tether's illegal activities in New York. These legal actions send a clear message that we will stand up to corporate greed whether it comes out of a traditional bank, a virtual currency trading platform, or any other type of financial institution."

Tether's Twitter response in regard to the lawsuit reminded me of when I was a kid who blatantly stole cookies from the cookie jar, yet when confronted about it by my parents, I would admit to no wrongdoing while my shirt was covered in cookie crumbs.

To continually push Bitcoin into the limelight, many renowned Bitcoin maximalists such as Anthony Pompliano (Founder and Partner at the hedge fund Morgan Creek Digital) and Dan Held (Director of Business Development at the exchange Kraken), will bite their tongues and take it to their grave before speaking an ill word of Bitcoin. They refuse to publicly acknowledge any sort of concern towards Tether in interviews or on their socials by claiming that any negative news regarding Tether is just "FUD" - fear, uncertainty and doubt. It's quite obvious they feed off on building Bitcoin as untouchable because Pomp profits off on the investors linked to his hedge fund and Held's job is literally to sell the dream of crypto to his prospective clients by working for a leading exchange. To dig into the topic of Tether's lawsuit further, I tried to reach out to Dan Held on Twitter to hear an "expert within the fields" opinion and he blocked me right away. This honestly made me laugh out loud.

I would have understood if I said something offensive, but I simply was asking for his honest opinion on the case and he childishly cut me out. By speaking to other investors online the same day, we discovered that there was a pattern in which he went on a massive blocking spree to anyone who brought up Tether. It's almost like he's trying to publicly paint a biased narrative about Bitcoin online...hmmm... not suspicious at all. That to me is another red flag since it's imperative for any investment to weigh the pros and cons and to not only chase the good news, but to soak in the negative as well to see if the risk is worth the reward.

From here on out, there are two paths that Tether can go down now due to the case in New York being closed. The lawsuit with the NYAG could set an example within the law and act as a ripple effect in other states and countries, which is the "ticking time bomb" that Buterin was referring to. Alternatively, since Tether is known for manipulating the price of Bitcoin, the powers that be could quite frankly encourage the coerced manipulation to continue propelling the price of Bitcoin to keep hitting an all-time high. Corruption has worked for the stock market in the past, so it's only fitting that there would be a puppet show of some sort within the crypto market as well, right?

Regardless of how innovative Bitcoin is, the pioneer crypto takes the element of power and control out of the hands of those who would rather be the puppeteer than the puppet. Therefore, it is imperative to take the above threats into consideration before investing to weigh the pros and cons. Some investors think these threats are utter bullshit and others take them seriously, so it's up for you to stay on track of any advancements and continue to do your own due diligence. I am simply trying to showcase both sides of the spectrum so it is essential for you to formulate your own opinion on this matter.

Although there is a dark shadow cast over Tether and Bitcoin, the cryptocurrency sector remains a bridge to financial freedom for the dedicated few who embark on this journey. The economic, business and financial systems are shifting before our very eyes and I expect the 2021 crypto bull market to shift the mainstream perception that decentralised finance is here to stay. The sector will turn heads like it has never done before and people will look back and wish they would have seized the opportunity to invest whatever pennies they could have scrapped together. By making an impact on our digital culture and well-being for the next decade, many people who rarely had an interest in crypto will suddenly perk up at the thought of buying or selling an NFT. In addition, millions of unbanked citizens in Africa will finally have financial security for the first time, everyday people can make a passive income from crypto interest rates, smart contracts will revolutionise the derivatives market and a new global reserve digital currency has the power to dethrone the American dollar. The shockingly part above all is that many retail investors will have the ability to climb up the wealth ladder to admirably gain financial freedom. There will of course be thrilling highs and there will be disastrous lows, however, those who are in it for the long haul and have strong hands will persevere. There will always be skeptics along the way, which is expected, but I can't seem to wipe the smug smirk off my face just thinking of how the next decade will be profitable due to the new quantum financial system.

At first glance, the sector seems like a scrambled 1000-piece puzzle since there are an overwhelming amount of tiny pieces that look awfully similar. Remember that it is easy to give up, but the more you focus section by section, your progress will allow you to see the bigger picture to get to the final result. As a final send off, ask yourself these questions: how do you plan to go from here on out? Do you feel inspired to do more research and take the dive into the wonderful world of crypto? Or will you be the one to put it off to the side and look back years from now and wish you would have taken the leap of faith? To invest or not to invest? That is the question. Which option will you choose?

Sources

'A Digital Currency Should Be Adopted as the World's Leading Reserve Currency'. *World*
   Economic Forum, https://www.weforum.org/agenda/2018/04/from-dolla r-to-e-sdr/

About Gematria | Yale University Library. https://web.library.yale.edu/catal oging/hebraica/about-gematria.

Altcoin Daily. *My Cryptocurrency Investing Strategy HAS CHANGED! Big Ethereum/Cardano Update!*. 2021, https://www.youtube.com/watch?v=uJJbk hzziQs.

'Altcoin Season Index: Is it Altseason right now?' *Blockchaincenter*, https://www.blockchaincenter.net/altcoin-season-index/.

ATTACHMENT A: STATEMENT OF FACTS AND VIOLATIONS . FinCEN, https://www.fincen.gov/sites/default/files/shared/Ripple_Facts.pdf.

Attorney General James Ends Virtual Currency Trading Platform Bitfinex's Illegal Activities in New York. https://ag.ny.gov/press-release/2021/attorne y-general-james-ends-virtual-currency-trading-platform-bitfinexs-illegal. Accessed 5 May 2021.

Austin, Sarah. 'The Digital Dollar's Global Potential For Entrepreneurship'. *Entrepreneur*, 15 Sept. 2020, https://www.entrepreneur.com/article/355707.

Bambrough, Billy. 'New ECB Boss Christine Lagarde Made A Serious Bitcoin Warning'. *Forbes*, https://www.forbes.com/sites/billybambrough/20 19/07/07/new-ecb-boss-christine-lagarde-made-a-serious-bitcoin-warnin g/. Accessed 5 May 2021.

Barber, Brad, et al. *Do Day Traders Rationally Learn About Their Ability?* Berkeley University, Oct. 2017, https://faculty.haas.berkeley.edu/odean/pa pers/Day%20Traders/Day%20Trading%20and%20Learning%2011021 7.pdf

Best, Richard, et al. *1:20-Cv-10832*. https://www.sec.gov/litigation/comp laints/2020/comp-pr2020-338.pdf.

'Biden's Treasury Pick Warns Cryptocurrency Poses Terrorism Risk'. *Fortune*, https://fortune.com/2021/01/19/janet-yellen-confirmation-bitcoi n-biden-treasury-nominee-cryptocurrency-warning-terrorism/. Accessed 17 May 2021.

BitBoy Crypto. *Raoul Pal on Ethereum: BIGGEST Opportunity in Crypto in 2021*. https://www.youtube.com/watch?v=IAqjrfnUDMc.

'Bitcoin Billionaire Cameron Winklevoss Says Ethereum Significantly Undervalued, DeFi Crypto Assets Are Just Getting Started'. *The Daily Hodl*, 8 Feb. 2021, https://dailyhodl.com/2021/02/08/bitcoin-billionaire-cameron-winklevoss-says-ethereum-significantly-undervalued-defi-crypto-assets-ar e-just-getting-started/.

Bitcoin Halving Dates History | StormGain. https://stormgain.com/blog/bit coin-halving-dates-history. Accessed 5 May 2021.

'Bitcoin Shortage Is Real, and PayPal Is the Cause, Pantera Capital Claims'. *Cointelegraph*, https://cointelegraph.com/news/bitcoin-shortage-is-real-an d-paypal-is-the-cause-pantera-capital-claims. Accessed 5 May 2021.

Cointelegraph, https://cointelegraph.com/news/bitcoin-shortage-is-real-a nd-paypal-is-the-cause-pantera-capital-claims. Accessed 17 May 2021.

'Bitcoin Will 10X Compared to Gold, Says JP Morgan'. *Crypto Briefing*, 26 Oct. 2020, https://cryptobriefing.com/bitcoin-will-10x-compared-gold-sa ys-jp-morgan/.

Bloomfield, Arthur I. (Arthur Irving) and Federal Reserve Bank of New York. *Monetary Policy Under the International Gold Standard: 1880-1914*. Federal Reserve Bank of New York, 1959.

Boyapati, Vijay. 'The Bullish Case for Bitcoin'. *Medium*, 22 Apr. 2021, https://vijayboyapati.medium.com/the-bullish-case-for-bitcoin-6ecc8bdec c1.

Brad Garlinghouse Says 99% of Cryptocurrencies Will 'Probably Go to Zero'. https://uk.finance.yahoo.com/news/brad-garlinghouse-says-99-cryptocurr encies-230033717.html. Accessed 5 May 2021.

'Can We Have A Single Global Currency?» Science ABC'. *Science ABC*, 19 Oct. 2020, https://www.scienceabc.com/social-science/can-we-have-a-sin gle-global-currency.html.

Capital, Pantera. 'Two Centuries Of Debt In One Month:: Pantera Blockchain Letter, July 2020'. *Medium*, 29 July 2020, https://blog.panter acapital.com/two-centuries-of-debt-in-one-month-pantera-blockchain-let ter-july-2020-f876b43448a2.

'Cardano (ADA) Will Outperform Ethereum 2.0 in DeFi Space –Charles Hoskinson'. *Herald Sheets*, 9 Feb. 2021, https://heraldsheets.com/cardano-a da-will-outperform-ethereum-2-0-in-defi-space-charles-hoskinson/.

'Cardano: IOG Reveals World's Largest Blockchain Deployment in Africa'. *Crypto News Flash*, 7 Feb. 2021, https://www.crypto-news-flash.com/carda no-iog-reveals-worlds-largest-blockchain-deployment-in-africa/.d

'Casting Light on Central Bank Digital Currencies'. *IMF*, https://www.imf .org/en/Publications/Staff-Discussion-Notes/Issues/2018/11/13/Casting-Light-on-Central-Bank-Digital-Currencies-46233. Accessed 5 May 2021.

Ceresney, Andrew, et al. *1:20-Cv-10832-AT* . storage.courtlistener.com/re-cap/gov.uscourts.nysd.551082/gov.uscourts.nysd.551082. 45.0.pdf

Chawaga, Peter. 'Stop The Bitcoin FUD: Criminal Cryptocurrency Transactions Are Falling'. *Bitcoin Magazine: Bitcoin News, Articles, Charts, and Guides*, https://bitcoinmagazine.com/business/stop-the-bitcoin-fud-crimin al-cryptocurrency-transactions-are-falling. Accessed 17 May 2021.

Cheah, Jeremy Eng-Tuck. 'What Is DeFi and Why Is It the Hottest Ticket in Cryptocurrencies?' *The Conversation*, http://theconversation.com/what-is-d efi-and-why-is-it-the-hottest-ticket-in-cryptocurrencies-144883. Accessed 5 May 2021.

'Citibank Executive Says Bitcoin Will Trade at $318,000 by End of 2021'. *Bitcoin News*, 16 Nov. 2020, https://news.bitcoin.com/citibank-executive-sa ys-bitcoin-will-trade-at-318000-by-end-of-2021/.

Bitcoin News, 16 Nov. 2020, https://news.bitcoin.com/citibank-executive-says-bitcoin-will-trade-at-318000-by-end-of-2021/.

Clifford, Catherine. 'Nearly 68% of the World's Richest People Are "self-

Made," Says New Report'. *CNBC*, 26 Sept. 2019, https://www.cnbc.com/20 19/09/26/majority-of-the-worlds-richest-people-are-self-made-says-new-report.html.

'Codius Is Open Source'. *Ripple*, 4 Aug. 2014, https://ripple.com/insights/ codius-is-open-source.

Coelho-Prabhu, Sid. *A Beginner's Guide to Decentralized Finance (DeFi)*. 6 Jan. 2020, https://blog.coinbase.com/a-beginners-guide-to-decentralized-fi nance-defi-574c68ff43c4.

Cointelegraph. *Institutional Money to Propel Bitcoin to over $250K in One Year? | Interview with Raoul Pal*. 2020, Institutional money to propel Bitcoin to over $250K in one year? | Interview with Raoul Pal.

Crypto Crime Summarized: Scams and Darknet Markets Dominated 2020 by Revenue, But Ransomware Is the Bigger Story. https://blog.chainalysis.com/re ports/2021-crypto-crime-report-intro-ransomware-scams-darknet-marke ts. Accessed 5 May 2021.

'Crypto Futures Exchange Bakkt Going Public at a Valuation of $2.1 Billion – Exchanges Bitcoin News'. *Bitcoin News*, 12 Jan. 2021, https://news.bitcoin. com/crypto-futures-exchange-bakkt-going-public-at-a-valuation-of-2-1-b illion/.

Crypto, What Is It Good For? An Overview of Cryptocurrency Use Cases. World Economic Forum , Dec. 2020, http://www3.weforum.org/docs/WEF_Cryp tocurrency_Uses_Cases_2020.pdf.

'Cryptocurrencies'. *World Economic Forum*, https://www.weforum.org/co mmunities/gfc-on-cryptocurrencies. Accessed 5 May 2021.

'Cryptocurrency Makes World Economic Forum's Davos Agenda'. *Coin-telegraph*, 24 Jan. 2021, https://cointelegraph.com/news/cryptocurrency-m akes-world-economic-forum-s-davos-agenda.

CryptoWhale. 'Ethereum's Buterin Says Tether Is Bitcoin's "Ticking Time Bomb Demon"'. *Medium*, 13 Mar. 2021, https://medium.com/the-capital/et hereums-buterin-says-tether-is-bitcoin-s-ticking-time-bomb-demon-9d21 38621145.

'Davos 2020 Will Have Impressive List of Speakers, Ripple CEO May Join'. *Coinspeaker*, 20 Jan. 2020, https://www.coinspeaker.com/davos-2020-spea

kers-ripple/.

Denning, Tim. 'The Biggest Wealth Transfer in History Is Happening Right Now'. *Medium*, 31 Aug. 2020, https://medium.com/the-ascent/the-biggest-wealth-transfer-in-history-is-happening-right-now-3826c09c6696.

Desjardins, Jeff. 'All of the World's Money and Markets in One Visualization'. *Visual Capitalist*, 27 May 2020, https://www.visualcapitalist.com/all-o f-the-worlds-money-and-markets-in-one-visualization-2020/.

Dewar, Phil. *Kendra Hill Archive* . https://threadreaderapp.com/thread/11 89356847117033484.html.

Digital Transformation and the Rise of Fintech: Blockchain, Bitcoin and Digital Finance 2021. JP Morgan, 18 Feb. 2021, https://www.tbstat.com/wp/upload s/2021/02/JPM_Bitcoin_Report.pdf.

Dovbnya, Alex. *Cardano (ADA) Just Made History by Surpassing XRP*. 2 July 2021, https://u.today/cardano-ada-just-made-history-by-surpassing-xrp.

'ECB Steps in over Swift's ISO 20022 Migration Delay'. *Finextra Research*, 5 May 2020, https://www.finextra.com/newsarticle/35764/ecb-steps-in-ov er-swifts-iso-20022-migration-delay.

Finextra Research, 5 May 2020, https://www.finextra.com/newsarticle/35 764/ecb-steps-in-over-swifts-iso-20022-migration-delay.

Edwards, John. 'Bitcoin's Price History'. *Investopedia*, investopedia.com/ar ticles/forex/121815/bitcoins-price-history.asp. Accessed 17 May 2021.

Englesson, Niclas, and Sid John Leopold . *ECO-FRIENDLY CURRENCIES*. Nov. 2017, https://www.stedas.hr/ripple/Eco-friendly-cryptocurrency.pdf.

Englesson, Niclas, and Sid John Leopold. *How Eco Friendly Is Our Money and Is There an Alternative?* http://papers.netrogenic.com/sid/eco-friendly-money.pdf.

'Environmental Cryptocurrency Mining vs. Consensus'. *Ripple*, 8 July 2020, https://ripple.com/insights/the-environmental-impact-cryptocurren cy-mining-vs-consensus/.

Ethereum. 'Reddit Announces Partnership with the Ethereum Foundation'. *R/Ethereum*, 27 Jan. 2021, reddit.com/r/ethereum/comments/l6c3kx/red dit_announces_partnership_with_the_ethereum.

'Ethereum - An Investigation'. *Real Vision*, https://www.realvision.com/sh

ows/the-interview-crypto/videos/ethereum-an-investigation/. Accessed 5 May 2021.

Ethereum's Buterin Says Tether Is Bitcoin's 'Ticking Time Bomb Demon'. https://cryptonews.com/news/ethereum-s-buterin-says-tether-is-bitco in-s-ticking-time-bom-9494.htm. Accessed 5 May 2021.

'EW Zero'. *Energy Web,* https://www.energyweb.org/technology/applicati ons/ew-zero/. Accessed 5 May 2021.

Exclusive: US Congress Members to Submit Major pro-Cryptocurrency Bill - Early Support Coming from Both Parties... https://www.globalcryptopress.c om/2019/01/exclusive-members-of-us-congress-from.html. Accessed 5 May 2021.

'Fact Checking The Infamous 1988 Economist Cover: "Get Ready for a World Currency"'. *Steemit,* 22 Dec. 2017, https://steemit.com/economist/@ subscription/fact-checking-the-infamous-1988-economist-cover-get-read y-for-a-world-currency.

Steemit, 22 Dec. 2017, https://steemit.com/economist/@subscription/fact -checking-the-infamous-1988-economist-cover-get-ready-for-a-world-cur rency.

FAQ - Bitcoin. https://bitcoin.org/en/faq#general. Accessed 17 May 2021.

'Federal Reserve Task Force: Ripple Improves Speed and Transparency of Global Payments'. *Ripple,* 21 July 2017, https://ripple.com/insights/federal- reserve-task-force-ripple-improves-speed-transparency-global-payments/.

'Former SEC Official Says There's a Good Chance Agency Loses Its Case Against Ripple and XRP – Here's Why'. *The Daily Hodl,* 4 Feb. 2021, https://d ailyhodl.com/2021/02/04/former-sec-official-says-theres-a-good-chance- agency-loses-its-case-against-ripple-and-xrp-heres-why/.

'Game Time? Microsoft Adopts Ethereum Blockchain for Gaming Royalties'. *Cointelegraph,* https://cointelegraph.com/news/game-time-micr osoft-adopts-ethereum-blockchain-for-gaming-royalties. Accessed 5 May 2021.

Get Ready for the Phoenix – The Reality of a One World Currency | Armstrong Economics. https://www.armstrongeconomics.com/international-news/p olitics/get-ready-for-the-phoenix-the-reality-of-a-one-world-currency/.

Accessed 5 May 2021.

Gibbons , Samuel, and Christopher Bendiksen . *The Bitcoin Mining Network - Trends, Composition, Average Creation Cost, Electricity Consumption & Sources* . 3 Dec. 2019, https://coinshares.com/assets/resources/Research/bitcoin-mining-network-december-2019.pdf.

'Global Crypto and FinTech Energy Sustainability'. *Ripple*, 30 Sept. 2020, https://ripple.com/insights/leading-the-way-on-global-crypto-and-fintech -sustainability/.

Grasping Large Numbers. https://www.ehd.org/science_technology_large numbers.php. Accessed 5 May 2021.

Griffin, John M., and Amin Shams. *Is Bitcoin Really Un-Tethered?* SSRN Scholarly Paper, ID 3195066, Social Science Research Network, 28 Oct. 2019. *papers.ssrn.com*, https://papers.ssrn.com/abstract=3195066.

Grothaus, Michael. 'Twitter Attack Update: 130 High-Profile Accounts Targeted, 400 Bitcoin Payments Made'. *Fast Company*, 17 July 2020, https://www.fastcompany.com/90529148/twitter-attack-update-130-high-profile-accounts-targeted-400-bitcoin-payments-made.

'Harvard Economics Professor: Governments Will Not Allow Bitcoin on a Big Scale and They Will Win – Regulation Bitcoin News'. *Bitcoin News*, 24 Jan. 2021, https://news.bitcoin.com/harvard-economics-professor-governments-will-not-allow-bitcoin-big-scale/.

'HOARDING OF GOLD'. *The New York Times*, 6 Apr. 1933. *NYTimes.com*, https://www.nytimes.com/1933/04/06/archives/hoarding-of-gold.html.

How Do You Explain The Mission Of Cardano? https://www.youtube.com/ watch?v=l_Nv0-PVrnM.

'How Is the International Money Transfer Market Evolving?' *Toptal Finance Blog*, toptal.com/finance/market-research-analysts/international-money-transfer. Accessed 5 May 2021.

How Many Bitcoins Are There? How Many Left to Mine? (2021). https://www.buybitcoinworldwide.com/how-many-bitcoins-are-there/#:~:text=How %20Many%20Bitcoins%20Are%20There%20Now%20in%20Circulation%3F ,when%20new%20blocks%20are%20mined. Accessed 5 May 2021.

I AM HODLING. https://bitcointalk.org/index.php?topic=375643.0.

Accessed 17 May 2021.

IMF's Lagarde: Disruptors like Cryptocurrencies Are 'clearly Shaking the System'. CNBC, 11 Apr. 2019, https://www.youtube.com/watch?v=zG 4IUHVN7bM.

'India and Nigeria's Crypto Crackdowns Continue Old Trends'. *CoinDesk*, 9 Feb. 2021, https://www.coindesk.com/india-and-nigerias-crypto-crackd owns-continue-old-trends.

Investing in Flare Networks. https://coil.com/p/xpring/Investing-in-Flare-Networks-/srIKao0Kf. Accessed 5 May 2021.

'IOHK on the Brink of Securing a Massive Cardano Government Contract in Africa'. *CryptoSlate*, 8 Feb. 2021, https://cryptoslate.com/iohk-on-the-bri nk-of-securing-a-massive-cardano-government-contract-in-africa/.

'Is Bitcoin the "New World Currency?" 1988 Article Prophecy???' *Steemit*, 12 Feb. 2018, https://steemit.com/bitcoin/@freetherobots/is-bitcoin-the-n ew-world-currency-1988-article-prophecy.

'ISO 20022 Is an Opportunity for UK Challenger Banks to Modernise Their Payment Infrastructure'. *PA Consulting*, https://www.paconsulting.co m/newsroom/expert-opinion/the-fintech-times-iso-20022-is-an-opportu nity-for-uk-challenger-banks-to-modernise-their-payment-infrastructure-18-december-2020/. Accessed 5 May 2021.

PA Consulting, https://www.paconsulting.com/newsroom/expert-opinion /the-fintech-times-iso-20022-is-an-opportunity-for-uk-challenger-banks-to-modernise-their-payment-infrastructure-18-december-2020/. Accessed 17 May 2021.

'ISO 20022 Migration – Everything You Need to Know'. *SWIFT - The Global Provider of Secure Financial Messaging Services*, https://www.swift.com /news-events/webinars/iso-20022-migration-everything-you-need-know. Accessed 5 May 2021.

Jan 31, Chris Markoch, et al. 'Stellar Lumens Is Worth Keeping An Eye On As Scarcity Should Drive Value'. *InvestorPlace*, 31 Jan. 2021, https://investor place.com/2021/01/stellar-lumens-should-increase-in-value/.

Jared. 'The Power of Dollar Cost Averaging into Bitcoin'. *Medium*, 29 June 2019, https://medium.com/predict/the-power-of-dollar-cost-averaging-in

to-bitcoin-2fad7fb12ce6.

'JP Morgan CEO Jamie Dimon: I'd Fire Trader "In a Second" for Trading Bitcoin'. *Money*, https://money.com/jp-morgan-ceo-jamie-dimon-id-fire-tr ader-in-a-second-for-trading-bitcoin/. Accessed 17 May 2021.

Kelleher, John P. 'Why Do Bitcoins Have Value?' *Investopedia*, https://www .investopedia.com/ask/answers/100314/why-do-bitcoins-have-value.asp. Accessed 17 May 2021.

'Kik Settles SEC Lawsuit for $5M over Its 2017 "Initial Coin Offering"'. *SiliconANGLE*, 22 Oct. 2020, https://siliconangle.com/2020/10/22/kik-sett les-sec-lawsuit-5m-2017-initial-coin-offering/.

Lagarde, Christine, and IMF Managing Director Singapore Fintech Festival. 'Winds of Change: The Case for New Digital Currency'. *IMF*, https://www.imf.org/en/News/Articles/2018/11/13/sp111418-winds-of-change-the-case-for-new-digital-currency. Accessed 5 May 2021.

Learn, Bybit. *What Is Cardano (ADA) and Is It a Good Investment? (2021)*. 25 Dec. 2020, https://learn.bybit.com/altcoins/what-is-cardano-ada-and-is-it-a-good-investment/#:~:text=One%20of%20the%20most%20significant,very %20popular%20among%20cryptocurrency%20enthusiasts.&text=All%20thi s%20and%20the%20latest,great%20profit%20to%20its%20investors.

Lipton, Alex, and Stuart Levi. 'An Introduction to Smart Contracts and Their Potential and Inherent Limitations'. *The Harvard Law School Forum on Corporate Governance*, 26 May 2018, https://corpgov.law.harvard.edu/2018/ 05/26/an-introduction-to-smart-contracts-and-their-potential-and-inhere nt-limitations/.

lizleafloor. *Symbolism of the Mythical Phoenix Bird: Renewal, Rebirth and Destruction*. https://www.ancient-origins.net/myths-legends/ancient-symb olism-magical-phoenix-002020. Accessed 17 May 2021.

Magazine, Bitcoin. 'Stellar's Jed McCaleb: What's New on the Upgraded Stellar Network'. *Bitcoin Magazine: Bitcoin News, Articles, Charts, and Guides*, https://bitcoinmagazine.com/business/stellar-s-jed-mccaleb-what-s-new-on-the-upgraded-stellar-network-1452109082. Accessed 5 May 2021.

March 2020, 18th. 'Swift's ISO 20022 Migration Set Back a Year to November 2022'. *FinTech Futures*, 18 Mar. 2020, https://www.fintechfu

tures.com/2020/03/swifts-iso-20022-migration-set-back-a-year-to-nove
mber-2022/.

'Mike Novogratz: Five Crypto Assets Could Replace JP Morgan and the
New York Stock Exchange'. *The Daily Hodl*, 1 Feb. 2021, https://dailyhodl.c
om/2021/02/01/mike-novogratz-five-crypto-assets-could-replace-jp-mor
gan-and-the-new-york-stock-exchange/.

Mix. 'Ripple's CTO Invented a Distributed Computer System 20 Years
before Blockchain – Ask Him about It'. *TNW | Hardfork*, 16 Aug. 2018,
https://thenextweb.com/news/blockchain-cryptocurrency-bitcoin-ripple.

'Ripple's CTO Invented a Distributed Computer System 20 Years before
Blockchain – Ask Him about It'. *TNW | Hardfork*, 16 Aug. 2018, https://then
extweb.com/news/blockchain-cryptocurrency-bitcoin-ripple.

Murray, Tom. '18 Times "The Simpsons" Accurately Predicted the Future'.
Business Insider, https://www.businessinsider.com/the-simpsons-is-good-at
-predicting-the-future-2016-11. Accessed 17 May 2021.

Nelson. 'Forget Satoshi Nakamoto, David Schwartz Is the Trillion Dollar
Man'. *XRP Ripple News*, 2 Dec. 2019, https://xrpripplenews.com/2019/12/0
2/forget-satoshi-nakamoto-david-schwartz-is-the-trillion-dollar-man/.

'Forget Satoshi Nakamoto, David Schwartz Is the Trillion Dollar Man'.
XRP Ripple News, 2 Dec. 2019, https://xrpripplenews.com/2019/12/02/forg
et-satoshi-nakamoto-david-schwartz-is-the-trillion-dollar-man/.

'Ripple & XRP Praised at OECD Global Blockchain Policy Conference'.
XRP Ripple News, 14 Sept. 2019, https://xrpripplenews.com/2019/09/14/ri
pple-xrp-praised-at-oecd-global-blockchain-policy-conference/.

*NEW SEC CHAIR'S COMMENTARY ON Ripple XRP Being a BRIDGE
CURRENCY in 2018 AS AN MIT PROFESSOR.* 2021, https://www.youtube.c
om/watch?v=0XPrwiZkolg.

News·September 4, John P. Njui·NEWSAltcoin NewsBlockchain
NewsCryptocurrency, and 2018·1 Min Read. *XRP Is The Most Eco-Friendly
and Sustainable Currency - Ethereum World News*. https://ethereumworldnew
s.com/xrp-is-the-most-eco-friendly-and-sustainable-currency/. Accessed 5
May 2021.

'Nigeria's Central Bank Orders Banks to Close Accounts of All Crypto

Users'. *CoinDesk*, 5 Feb. 2021, https://www.coindesk.com/nigerias-central-bank-orders-banks-to-close-accounts-of-all-crypto-users.

'Now Is the Time for a "Great Reset"'. *World Economic Forum*, https://www.weforum.org/agenda/2020/06/now-is-the-time-for-a-great-reset/. Accessed 5 May 2021.

October 13, Matthew Braga and 2016. 'Meet the Wunderkind Developing the Blockchain Future of Business'. *Canadian Business - Your Source For Business News*, 13 Oct. 2016, https://www.canadianbusiness.com/innovatio n/change-agent/vitalik-buterin-ethereum/.

OVERALL KEY MILESTONES TO ENSURE A SUCCESSFUL BIG-BANG MIGRATION IN NOVEMBER 2021. European Central Bank , 28 May 2020, https://www.ecb.europa.eu/paym/pdf/consultations/Overall_key_milesto nes_to_ensure_a_successful_big-bang_migration_in_November_2021.pdf.

Ownership | Economist Group. https://www.economistgroup.com/results_ and_governance/ownership.html. Accessed 5 May 2021.

. https://www.economistgroup.com/results_and_governance/ownership. html. Accessed 17 May 2021.

PoolTogether. 'PoolTogether'. *PoolTogether*, https://pooltogether.com. Accessed 5 May 2021.

Purdy, Jack, and Ryan Watkins. *Bitcoin's Third Hlaving: Investment Theses and Implications* . Messari, https://messari.io/pdf/bitcoin-halving-2020-exp lained.pdf.

Quinn , Shannon. *What Is Bitcoin? A Beginner's Guide to Cryptocurrency.* 24 Jan. 2020, https://moneywise.com/investing/investing-basics/what-is-bitc oin-a-beginners-guide-to-cryptocurrency.

'Resetting Digital Currencies (Option 1)'. *World Economic Forum*, https://www.weforum.org/events/the-davos-agenda-2021/sessions/resetting-digital -currencies/. Accessed 5 May 2021.

'Ripple Case Study – Amazon Web Services (AWS)'. *Amazon Web Services, Inc.*, https://aws.amazon.com/partners/success/ripple/. Accessed 5 May 2021.

Ripple CEO Cautions Public Companies Against Holding Bitcoin. 11 Sept. 2020, https://u.today/ripple-ceo-cautions-public-companies-against-holdi

ng-bitcoin?amp&__twitter_impression=true.

'Ripple Looks for a New Director to Convince Central Banks on XRP Benefits'. *Invezz*, 23 Nov. 2020, https://invezz.com/news/2020/11/23/rippl e-looks-for-a-new-director-to-convince-central-banks-on-xrp-benefits/.

'Ripple Smart Contracts Creator Targets Ethereum with New Tech Launch'. *CoinDesk*, 6 June 2018, https://www.coindesk.com/ripple-smart-contracts- creator-targets-ethereum-new-tech-launch.

'Ripple to Become the Amazon of Crypto By 2025: Brad Garlinghouse'. *Bitcoinist.Com*, 17 Feb. 2020, https://bitcoinist.com/ripple-to-become-the-a mazon-of-crypto-by-2025-brad-garlinghouse/.

'Rishi Sunak Launches Taskforce on Bank of England Digital Currency'. *The Guardian*, 19 Apr. 2021. *www.theguardian.com*, http://www.theguardian. com/business/2021/apr/19/rishi-sunak-bank-of-england-digital-currency- uk-brexit-eu.

Ross, Sean. 'What It Would Take for the U.S. Dollar to Collapse'. *Investopedia*, https://www.investopedia.com/articles/forex-currencies/091416/what -would-it-take-us-dollar-collapse.asp. Accessed 5 May 2021.

Schwartz, David. *What Is the Difference between XRP and RippleNet?* https://www.quora.com/What-is-the-difference-between-XRP-and-Ripple Net.

'SEC to Establish a Node on XRP Ledger – Ripple's Executive VP'. *NewsLogical*, 27 Jan. 2020, https://newslogical.com/sec-to-establish-a-node- on-xrp-ledger-ripples-executive-vp/.

Shams, Amin, and John Griffin. *Is Bitcoin Really Un-Tethered?* Oct. 2019, https://papers.ssrn.com/sol3/papers.cfm?abstract_id=3195066.

Staff, Reuters. 'Saudi Arabia's Central Bank Signs Blockchain Deal with Ripple'. *Reuters*, 15 Feb. 2018. *www.reuters.com*, https://www.reuters.com/ar ticle/us-saudi-cenbank-currency-idUSKCN1FZ0LD.

'Stellar Becomes New Home of USDC as Integration Goes Live'. *Cointelegraph*, https://cointelegraph.com/news/stellar-becomes-new-home-of-usd c-as-integration-goes-live. Accessed 5 May 2021.

'Stellar Strategist: Circle's USDC Issuance Opens Doors for DeFi'. *Crypto News Flash*, 6 Feb. 2021, https://www.crypto-news-flash.com/stellar-strate

gist-circles-usdc-issuance-opens-doors-for-defi/.

Stellar: XLM Could ROCKET in 2021, Here's Why!! 2020, https://www.you tube.com/watch?v=-hu-7kXYrGI&t=768s.

'The Difference Between Blockchain and Distributed Ledger Technology'. *TradeIX*, 30 Jan. 2018, https://tradeix.com/distributed-ledger-technology/.

'The Flare Network'. *Flare Networks*, 10 Aug. 2020, https://blog.flare.xyz/t he-flare-network/.

The Future of Currency in a Digital World . IMF F&D Magazine, June 2018, https://www.imf.org/external/pubs/ft/fandd/2018/06/pdf/fd0618.pdf.

'The Simpsons' Secret Formula: It's Written by Maths Geeks'. *The Guardian*, 21 Sept. 2013, http://www.theguardian.com/tv-and-radio/2013/sep/22/th e-simpsons-secret-formula-maths-simon-singh.

. *The Guardian*, 21 Sept. 2013, http://www.theguardian.com/tv-and-radi o/2013/sep/22/the-simpsons-secret-formula-maths-simon-singh.

'The World Economic Forum'. *World Economic Forum*, https://www.wefor um.org/. Accessed 17 May 2021.

Thread by @dewar_phil: 1/ In This Thread, I'd like to Introduce the XRP Community on CT to Kendra Hill, Another Alleged XRP Insider. Note That It's NOT Her Real Na.... https://threadreaderapp.com/thread/11893568471170 33484.html. Accessed 17 May 2021.

'Token Taxonomy Act to Address Blockchain, Innovation Flight in America'. *Congressman Warren Davidson*, 9 Apr. 2019, https://davidson.house.gov/201 9/4/token-taxonomy-act-address-blockchain-innovation-flight-america.

'TOP 5 Facts about Cryptocurrencies Which You Should Know! | Tokeneo'. *Tokeneo News - Everything about Cryptocurrencies*, 30 June 2020, https://toke neo.com/top-5-facts-about-cryptocurrencies-which-you-should-know/.

Tran, Decrypt /. Matt Hussey, Ki Chong. 'What Is Synthetix? A 3-Minute Guide to the Trading Platform'. *Decrypt*, 29 Apr. 2020, https://decrypt.co/re sources/what-is-synthetix-explained-ethereum-trading-learn.

UK Central Bank Chief Sees Digital Currency Displacing US Dollar as Global Reserve. https://uk.finance.yahoo.com/news/uk-central-bank-chief-sees-20 1715816.html. Accessed 5 May 2021.

https://uk.finance.yahoo.com/news/uk-central-bank-chief-sees-201715

816.html. Accessed 17 May 2021.

Untitled. https://bitcoin.org/en/faq#general.

https://www.ecb.europa.eu/paym/pdf/consultations/Overall_key_milest
ones_to_ensure_a_successful_big-bang_migration_in_November_2021.pd
f.

'USD Coin (USDC) Goes Live on the Stellar Blockchain'. *Crypto News Flash*, 2 Feb. 2021, https://www.crypto-news-flash.com/usd-coin-usdc-goes-live-on-the-stellar-blockchain/.

Walia, Arjun. *Did A 1988 Economist Magazine Predict A Bitcoin Explosion In 2018?* https://www.collective-evolution.com/2018/01/04/did-this-1988-ec onomist-magazine-predict-a-bitcoin-explosion-in-2018/. Accessed 5 May 2021.

Warren, Sheila, and Sumedha Deshmukh. '4 Predictions for Blockchain in 2021 – from Money to Art'. *World Economic Forum*, 3 Feb. 2021, https://www .weforum.org/agenda/2021/02/four-predictions-for-blockchain-in-2021/.

'WEF "Resetting Digital Currencies" Panelists Reveal Reasons for Cryp-tocurrency Reticence'. *BeInCrypto*, 29 Jan. 2021, https://beincrypto.com/we f-resetting-digital-currencies-panelists-reveal-reasons-for-cryptocurrency-reticence/.

'What Is Ethereum?' *Ethereum.Org*, https://ethereum.org. Accessed 5 May 2021.

'What Is the Paris Climate Agreement and Why Did the US Rejoin?' *BBC News*, 22 Apr. 2021. *www.bbc.co.uk*, https://www.bbc.com/news/science-en vironment-35073297.

White Paper | Diem Association. https://www.diem.com/en-us/white-pape r/. Accessed 5 May 2021.

https://www.diem.com/en-us/white-paper/. Accessed 17 May 2021.

Why Are People In Venezuela Starving (Hyperinflation Explained)? 2018, https://www.youtube.com/watch?v=ah9i3R9pRpg.

Working Money Channel. *Ripple XRP: Glenn Hutchins Describes Exactly What Ripple's Strategy Is At Davos 2021.* 2021, https://www.youtube.com/wa tch?v=zEo7zSjT1ag&feature=youtu.be.

Notes

Notes

Notes

Notes

Notes

Printed in Great Britain
by Amazon